AN EMPATH

The Empowered Empath

Quick & Easy

OWNING, EMBRACING AND MANAGING YOUR SPECIAL GIFTS

Rose Rosetree

Women's Intuition Worldwide
Sterling, Virginia

The Empowered Empath — Quick & Easy

OWNING, EMBRACING AND MANAGING YOUR GIFTS

Empath Empowerment® with Rose Rosetree, Series Book Two. Quick & Easy Edition of *The Empowered Empath*. Adapted from *Empowered by Empathy: 25 Ways to Fly in Spirit*; 1st printing 2001; 2nd printing 2005, revised; 3rd printing 2006, 4th printing 2010.

Empath Empowerment® is Rose Rosetree's unique system for helping empaths to improve quality of life, using techniques for appropriate positioning of consciousness, a system to help people born with one or more gifts as an empath.

PUBLISHER'S CATALOGING-IN-PUBLICATION

Rosetree, Rose.

Empowered empath — quick & easy : owning, embracing and managing your gifts / Rose Rosetree.

TO COME pages ; 14 x 21.59 centimeters cm. — (An Empath Empowerment® Books series ; book 2)

Issued also a full-length edition and as an ebook.

Includes bibliographical references and index in an online supplement.

ISBN-13: 978-1-935214-37-3 ISBN-10: 1-935214-37-3

1. Empathy. 2. Intuition. 3. Sensitivity (Personality trait) 4. Self-actualization (Psychology) 5. Aura. 6. Self-help techniques. 7. Consciousness. I. Adaptation of (work) Rosetree, Rose. Empowered by empathy, 25 ways to fly in spirit. II. Title.

BF575.E55 R67 2014 158/.2

ISBN: 978-1-935214-37-3

LCCN: 2014948705

Please direct all correspondence and inquiries to

Women's Intuition Worldwide, LLC
116 Hillsdale Drive, Sterling, VA 20164-1201
rights@rose-rosetree.com
703-450-9514

Visit our website: www.rose-rosetree.com

Dedication

Drip. Drip. Drip. In the apartment where you live, the faucet leaks. It always has.

That kitchen sink overflows, making puddles, causing a mess.

Shoes get wet a lot. Fine, you can cope with that. But mysterious problems happen too, like how your bedroom slippers sometimes get wet.

Really the answer is simple. Certain nights you get up for a midnight snack and you're thinking "Food" not "Puddles." Slippers get wet from that totally forgettable trip to the kitchen. Later you notice how your bedroom slippers have developed patches of wetness. It creeps you out.

Strange new problems come up all the time. You complain to your best friend, "There's a horrible smell of mold in my apartment. And I can't stop that leaky kitchen faucet from dripping."

"Just turn it off. That's what I do." says your friend.

This advice doesn't help one bit. What are you supposed to do now? You cope on your own, that's what.

So you place fans in certain strategic places. You figure out how to use hairdryers for a quick fix. Certain skin lotions help better than others for dealing with all your rashes from all the dampness.

In the back of your mind, you are constantly monitoring all that dampness.

Look, this faucet analogy is not about some hypothetical person and a hopeless problem. It's about you.

You may have a fairly common problem that afflicts 1 in 20 people. That problem is being born as an empath.

Your lifelong talent can be so special, helpful, delightful, embraceable... provided that you learn how to use it with skill. Being born with empath ***talent*** is different from having ***skill.*** All empaths are born talented. Skills must be learned. That's what you can learn here. You'll be able to learn just fine.

Really, it's a privilege, having the equivalent of an extra faucet in your kitchen sink. I will help you learn how to work that faucet.

As a result, you will stop having certain problems. You certainly won't have to work so hard at coping. If you have been blaming yourself, soon you'll stop. Every empath's faucet is installed dripping. That's just how they're made.

Guess what else? The liquid from your special empath's faucet is magnificent. Think fine wine. Think a really superb kind of vino that you could use for personal entertaining and even decant at work, gaining ever-greater prestige and success.

You see, what you have is the equivalent of an ***extra*** faucet in your home. Your empath talent is precious. I'm going to help you to own this very human talent of yours, then embrace it and manage it... to support every other good thing about your life.

Table of Contents

Table of Empath Gifts

Techniques Designed for Empath Empowerment®

1. *Hey, You.* To Become Conscious of Your Consciousness. — CHAPTER 26
2. *I Like.* Breaks the Power of Identification with Other People. — CHAPTER 27
3. *Install an Automatic Subconscious Alert.* Use Breath and Eyes to Interrupt Prolonged Unskilled Empath Merge. — CHAPTER 28
4. *Intro to Vibe-Raising Breaths.* Become More Present, Awake, Relaxed. — CHAPTER 29
5. *Introduction to Grounding Breaths.* Release Stress. And Maybe Also Become More Physically Aware. — CHAPTER 30
6. *A Human-Reality App for Grounding Breaths.* Transition Wisely from Spiritual Practices, Preventing Unskilled Empath Merges. — CHAPTER 31
7. *Get Big.* Make Divine Connection both Effective and Effortless. — CHAPTER 33
8. *Empath's First Aid.* Remove Imported STUFF. — CHAPTER 34
9. *Coming Home.* The Single Most Important Way to Improve Life for Any Empath. — CHAPTER 36

PART ONE

Owning Your Empath Gifts

An EMPATH is someone with at least one significant gift for directly experiencing what it is like to be another person. Many different empath gifts are possible, but the process of developing empath skill is identical whether you were born with one empath gift or many.

Whichever of these 15 special empath gifts you have, it was installed on the day you were born. Installed fully switched ON.

Don't just cope with that special talent. Make it work for you. I can teach you how, and it won't take much effort.

In fact, a skilled empath works way less hard than somebody who never learned this skill set.

Most unskilled empaths work very hard indeed. Maybe that includes you.

- Some empaths create their own workarounds, like using hairdryers in the dripping faucet analogy.
- Some empaths have created support groups, or found help online where they share tips and tricks to help them cope.
- Some empaths have studied with experts who don't prevent problems but, instead, help empaths adjust to the problems that come from being unskilled.
- All this can keep an empath busy and hopeful. Very busy, yet still unskilled.

Skill! Have you noticed how I keep using that word SKILL?

What kind of skill matters for an empath?

Not psychological boundary work or anything about behavior. Not energy work to clean up the mess from being an unskilled empath. Not avoiding energies of negative or overwhelming people. (With appropriate skill, an empath can go anywhere while remaining energetically protected.)

The kind of skill empaths need comes from using your AWARENESS, a gentle way of being awake inside. Ever since you were born, all your waking hours, you have had awareness.

That subtle yet dependable awareness is there for you every single day of your life, available once you wake up and think something like, "Hello, earth. Here I go again."

Thanks to awareness, you know whatever you know. You see whatever you see. You feel whatever you feel.

What, you already know about awareness?

Some of you empaths may have spent years actively exploring awareness (a.k.a. consciousness). Maybe you learned about it through yoga or meditation or prayer. All that experience can make it extra easy to learn empath skills.

Alternatively, you might have learned about awareness through studying energy. Maybe you learned Reiki. Or explored intuitive development. Or you work religiously with your angels. Or you work religiously at an Official Religion. Or you get along just fine with your own brand of disorganized religion.

With all due respect, none of that is expressly designed to help empaths, so put it aside for now. Prepare for success by bringing BEGINNER'S MIND, exploring as if for the first time. Trust your regular, everyday awareness. It is an amazing resource, ever fresh.

What if you are a beginner at anything about awareness?

No worries. You're starting clean and I'll teach you clean.

Being born as an empath doesn't mean that you have to like far-out New Age anything. So far you may have resisted Energy Talk with all your might. Well, becoming a skilled empath doesn't have to change that, not much.

What will I give you? Practical knowledge about energy. That will have to include some technical terms, used precisely, because I think like an engineer in this field. Rest assured, techie terms that will be introduced to you — they are no weirder than the word "Internet."

What won't I give you? Unnecessary extras. No radically changing your lifestyle or asking you to wear crystals or start channeling a ghost who claims to be a big deal from back in Atlantis.

Empath skills are simply skills. Like learning to tie your shoelaces or use a mobile phone.

CHAPTER 1

Different Empath Gifts, Different Problems

MALLED is one word for it, that strangely mutilated psychic state that some of us suffer after a trip to the mall. Emily always gets malled. Returning home after a shopping trip, she feels like an emotional basket case. No wonder she usually stays home instead.

"How can kids hang out at the malls just for fun?" Emily sighs.

(Note: Quotations throughout this book come from memory. Anecdotes are true, just not reported with court transcript accuracy. Also, first names used here are fictitious unless paired with last names. The dialogues in upcoming Q&A sections will be either reconstructed or fictitious, based on my experience teaching Empath Empowerment.)

Back at Emily, it isn't so much that she's curious how kids handle the malls. More like she's trying to divert attention. "How can kids hang out at the malls just for fun?"

It's hard for Emily not to blame herself. Millions of people — most people so far as she knows — don't find shopping a major ordeal. So what's wrong with her?

Talent as an empath is the problem, talent that Emily hasn't yet learned to use on purpose.

Many unskilled empaths interpret their talent negatively, inappropriately calling themselves names like "Over-sensitive," "Neurotic," or "Co-dependent." Ridiculous, Brave Empath! You have a gift. It's tricky but, with skill, you can purposely use that gift to fly in spirit.

Brave Empath, that is what I will be calling you in this book as I coach you in empath skills.

You are brave. Otherwise you wouldn't have been attracted to this system for helping empaths. Plenty of other books exist to console empaths who feel like victims. It takes uncommon courage to embrace who you are, to pursue skills that can abolish empath-related suffering, and to claim the leadership role that is rightfully yours.

Yes, leadership role. Of all the skill sets I teach, Empath Empowerment is my very favorite because that leadership is so important. Granted, before you gain skills as an empath, you may not feel much like a leader at all. You might feel more like John.

A Second Example of Being an Unskilled Empath

John first discovered his talent as an empath one lovely spring morning in 1994. He woke up feeling suicidal. "Don't get me wrong," John told me afterwards. "I have my ups and downs like everyone else. But this feeling was different.

"For years Greg has been my hero at the newspaper where we work. You could call him my mentor. That morning, a friend of ours called me to say that Greg was in bad shape. The day before, I wasn't at work. Greg was. And apparently the pressure got to him.

"He walked into the newsroom and lost control. You know those things that you can say to people, the things that are true but unforgivable? Well, he said them all.

"The morning after, Greg didn't know how to go on. So those suicidal feelings I was noticing? They belonged to him, not me.

"Eventually Greg managed to pull himself together. The feelings passed for us both. But I'll never forget that episode because it served as a kind of initiation.

Ever since, I have known that I had empath talent. Every day I connect to other people's pain. I have learned to accept this. Only I sure wish I could use my empath talent for happy things, too."

That's where empath skills make such a difference. You don't have to pick up other people's pain. You don't have to accept this as a necessary consequence of being sensitive.

Brave Empath, skills can make the difference. With skills of EMPATH EMPOWERMENT®, it will become a habit to keep your empath gifts turned OFF.

That's right, skills expressly designed to help empaths. This will allow you to break the drip-drip-drip habit of having empath gifts perpetually turned ON.

Afterwards I can teach you dedicated techniques to turn your empath gifts ON — at will — with Skilled Empath Merge. That use of your gifts can take you deeper and bigger and clearer than ever before. This is a skill when you purposely fly in spirit. Technically you know what you're doing. And how to do it. Who chooses when to turn that experience OFF or ON? You alone.

My name for that kind of experience is **SKILLED EMPATH MERGE.** Which sure is a contrast to what unskilled empaths do (including me back in the day).

Not only are an unskilled empath's gifts habitually turned ON. Innumerable times each day, that talented empath slips into Unskilled Empath Merge. Most of these are subconscious, superquick travels in consciousness; later you'll be learning about the various types.

Various types? Yes, you read that right. Moreover, each unskilled empath merge adds up to that drip-drip-drip kind of helplessness you may know all too well. Soon you will learn about different types of unskilled empath merge and, especially, you will learn how to prevent them. So fear not. Your life is about to become so much easier.

- I will show you how to stop those unskilled empath merges.
- Later I can help you learn to do the safe, skilled kind.
- Afterwards some lifestyle suggestions can be useful.

Note the order, Brave Empath. Because it is much more common for empaths to be offered lifestyle suggestions only. In my opinion, that puts the cart before the horse.

Actually, there isn't any horse. How useful is it, attempting lifestyle changes before you get basic empath skills? That doesn't work very well, except for providing an interesting hobby. Do you really need a never-ending form of psychological busywork?

Ha, I thought not. By contrast, effective skills will require relatively little time and take zero effort.

A Third Example of Being an Unskilled Empath

Back at examples of real-life empath students, let's turn to William. He suffered from problems related to a different form of empath talent than Emily's or John's. Until recently, William blamed himself for being a hypochondriac.

"I would go into a business meeting and come out with weird ailments. For years I thought I was making this up. Eventually I realized the aches and pains were real, only they belonged to other people, not me.

"A woman where I work suffers from migraines. When they start to hit, this woman, Ellen, is in such denial about her body, she has no clue. By the time she notices anything wrong, her headache has become a full-blown migraine and so she has to go to the emergency room.

"Finally I connected all this with me. When we're together at work and her symptoms start, who else gets a headache? Me. It's her headache but I'm sharing it.

"Sound crazy? Then get what we do now! At *my* first sign of a headache, I call Ellen and say, '*You* have a headache. Go take your medicine.' Now it never gets to the point where she has to go to the hospital.

"Great, I'm glad to help Ellen. But she never pays me to be her doctor or headache wearer. How can I stop taking on people's physical symptoms when I don't want to?"

Many so-called "hypochondriacs" are really volunteers who connect empathically with other people's health problems. Having a gift for receiving this kind of information becomes far more enjoyable when you learn to use the on-and-off switch.

Altogether, wishing to have control over your empath talent is healthy. Just because you have a gift doesn't mean you must be a slave to it, perpetually on call. The solution is to use empath talent in a way that empowers you.

Most empaths don't have experiences as extreme as those of William, John, or Emily. On the other hand, you may be misinterpreting pesky problems in your life due to unskilled empath talent. Undoubtedly you're underestimating the joys of using your empath gifts on purpose.

Curious about Empowerment?

Whatever makes you curious about being an empath, there's one thing you have in common with my other students: Talent that deserves to be nurtured.

There is no one talent or type of problem that all empaths have. So maybe you're wondering:

- How can I tell for sure if I am an empath?
- What are the different empath gifts, and which do I have?
- How can I learn to switch my empath gifts OFF for most of the time?
- How can different techniques switch my empath gifts ON most strongly?
- How can I best protect myself as an empath?

- I sense that living as an empath could be the basis for important kinds of spiritual service. Is that true? How can I do that more? How can I do that safely?

I'll help you to answer these questions and more with this Empath Empowerment Series. *The Empowered Empath — Quick & Easy,* will help you to answer Questions 1, 2, 3, and 5. *The Master Empath* will provide juicy answers to the two remaining questions, information that must come later.

This sequence for learning will make sense to you if you agree with sayings like "You've got to walk before you can run."

One thing's for sure. If you're reading this book, it's a little late to choose whether or not you would like to *be* an empath. Assuming that you're reading of your own free will, chances are that you qualify — although probably not yet as a *skilled* empath.

I'm glad to help. Systematically I will help you to develop Empath Empowerment, skills that have helped thousands of empaths before you, with results that have ranged from merely satisfying to downright transformational.

CHAPTER 2

Empath Quiz

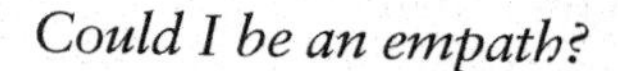

Could I be an empath?

It's a fair question, especially since 95 people out of 100 aren't. Yes, 5% is my ballpark estimate for the number of adults, living now, who are naturally gifted as empaths.

But you don't need to know statistics, not nearly so much as you need to know about you. The following quiz can help.

Empath Quiz
THE QUICK QUESTIONNAIRE

Empaths can fly... in consciousness. Many times each day an unskilled empath will shift into another person's way of experiencing life, whether physically, mentally, emotionally, or spiritually. Do you have talent as an empath? Here's a quick aptitude test.

Answer **TRUE** or **FALSE**.

1. When I'm with people who interest me, I wish I knew what it was like to be them. **T F**

2. It annoys (or amuses) me when people put on a show of being very tuned into others and I can tell that they're really not. **T F**

3. I'm thin-skinned about other people, not just myself. **T F**

4. One of the best parts of falling in love, for me, is seeing the world through my lover's eyes. Everything becomes different and new. **T F**

5. Of all the compliments I have received, some of my favorites are variations on, "You really answer my questions." and "You understand me better than others do." T F

6. When with different friends, I don't just talk to them. My whole wavelength shifts. For example, when I'm with an artist, colors look brighter than usual; when with a musician, I'm more aware of sounds; when with an athlete, I feel more physically vibrant. T F

7. If I have to give the same speech to three different strangers, it comes out differently each time. Somehow I sense information that causes me to adjust the words automatically. With a highly educated listener, for instance, I find myself using longer words — even if nobody has told me that this person is highly educated. T F

8. When in the presence of somebody who is ill, it takes no effort for me to experience some of what that person is going through. In fact, if I were to let myself go, my experience of that person's illness could be overwhelming. T F

9. In certain situations (e.g., Talking or dancing or teaching), I get right on another person's wavelength — how he or she thinks. This kind of sharing is very special to me. T F

10. I don't just talk to my plants. I feel like they talk back to me. T F

11. Energetically it is freeing for me to be outdoors, and more than a change of scene. The way I think and feel changes, as though I pick up on different kinds of consciousness expressed in animals and plants, or the landscape itself. T F

12. During times of closeness with my pet, I enter my pet's world. For me, that's the truly fascinating part of having a pet. **T F**

13. Looking in the mirror shocks me. "That's supposed to be me?" Truth is, I identify with being a (non-physical) energy presence more than identifying with this one particular face and body. **T F**

14. Friendship, for me, goes far beyond sharing common interests. I enjoy that my friends show me different ways to be. **T F**

15. I have a longing to connect with other people who are seeking a deeper dimension to life. Whenever I encounter these kindred spirits, I feel a kind of relief. Even if our paths cross only long enough to make quick eye contact, that chance meeting can lighten my spirit for hours. **T F**

Empath Quiz. ANSWERS

Brave Empath, if you answered yes to even one of these questions, you are probably a *natural* empath. And you will love how your life changes when you become a *skilled* empath.

Consider yourself well prepared for our survey of empath gifts in future chapters. That will help you tell for sure if you are an empath and, specifically, which empath gift(s) you have.

Empath Quiz. Q&A

Q. *I feel so validated already. What a relief to know I'm an empath. Isn't this all I need, really?*

A. If all you care about is a label for yourself, sure stop here. But this Program for Empath Empowerment can actually change your life. Consider that you have just tasted a tiny sample of the benefits to come.

Q. *How come folks don't usually talk about this? My favorite part of having a pet and all that. Usually if I tried to explain this kind of thing, I'd get tongue-tied.*

A. Understandably so. The *essence* of being an empath is to move in and out of deep experiences of consciousness. Yet everyday experiences, and problems, for an empath are very human. In developing this Empath Quiz, I sought ways to put a human face on those abstract, deep experiences.

Q. *Why expect a skeptic like me to be persuaded by such a general questionnaire?*

A. A better goal for yourself might be self-recognition, rather than persuasion.

Remember, an empath is someone with at least one significant gift for directly experiencing what it is like to be another person. Just one gift is enough to make you an empath. If you happen to be an empath, this Program for Empath Empowerment can greatly improve your life.

What is the purpose of this quiz or any quiz about whether you are an empath? Motivating you to explore this program. That's how you will discover the benefits.

CHAPTER 3

Since You're In, Let's Get Technical

A **Program for Empath Empowerment** is built right into this book. In this self-paced manual, you will learn two of the three steps for becoming a skilled empath.

Strictly speaking, only the first two steps are required for becoming a skilled empath. They can change your quality of life more than any skill set you have ever learned, like finally learning how to turn that water faucet OFF, ending the drip-drip-drip.

The third step of Empath Empowerment is optional. For that systematic sequence of instruction, turn to the next book of this series, The Master Empath. Survival skills first, entertainment later! Survival skills for an empath are exactly what you will get from this part of our Program for Empath Empowerment.

This won't be as hard as learning Chinese. More like working a new app. Let's take it one techie term at a time.

Techie Term 1. Empath

An **Empath** is someone with at least one significant gift for directly experiencing what it is like to be another person.

Although you may have many different empath gifts, all of them switch ON or OFF the same way. So empath skill is developed the same way whether you have been born with one empath gift or many.

Altogether I have identified 15 different empath gifts. Whichever ones you happen to have, they were installed on the day you were born. Installed fully switched ON.

What happens after that? Up to you.

Techie Term 2. Skilled Empath Merge

Before you gain control over this aspect of your life, unskilled empath merges happen many times every day, a kind of flying in spirit that may feel good sometimes. Although Emily, John, and William didn't especially enjoy doing this, you might have. Even if later you have always paid a price.

The purpose of this book is to help you stop paying that price.

Techie Term 3. STUFF

STUFF is a practical term used in Rosetree Energy Spirituality (RES) for stored-up energetic garbage. These are blobs and globs of astral-level energy, deposited within your aura in a way that causes confusion for your subconscious mind.

All the healing skill sets I teach have this in common: They aim to remove STUFF permanently. In fact, my motto as an emotional and spiritual healer is this: "STUFF can always, always, always be healed."

To make that healing permanent, STUFF removal must be followed by energetic **PUT IN.** That means adding subconscious energies and conscious knowledge which, together, awaken a stronger soul expression. Facilitating that kind of healing is my main area of professional expertise.

Preventing and removing STUFF related to being an empath will not solve other STUFF-related problems. However, it is a big deal to rid yourself of the type of STUFF that clobbers unskilled empaths. This particular type of STUFF has its very own name...

Techie Term 4. Imported STUFF

This Program for Empath Empowerment addresses **IMPORTED STUFF**. Which means STUFF belonging to *other people* that lands in *your* aura as a result of unskilled empath merge.

Once you learn how to banish Imported STUFF, your energy field will be naturally cleaner. Subconsciously, living this way is such a relief.

Noticing benefits will not require that you scrutinize your energies, either. In human terms, you'll find results. What can happen, just because you have vanquished Imported STUFF? For starters:

- Greater effectiveness at work or in school
- Establishing a stronger sense of identity
- Enjoying relationships more
- Greater personal power
- Spiritual awakening, living more in the present

You see, Brave Empath, Imported STUFF is really a bigger deal than some faucet that goes drip-drip-drip. That hidden energetic debris clutters up your subconscious mind and energy field in random ways, at random times, through problem energies belonging to random people.

No wonder being an unskilled empath is way confusing, both subconsciously and consciously.

No wonder empath skills can transform your life.

CHAPTER 4

Positioning Your What?

Position Your Consciousness. That's what.

Awareness, or consciousness, flows. You're so good at having awareness that it flows from the moment you first wake up until you drop off into Snoozeland.

All your waking hours, consciousness is positioned in one direction or another.

No need to be self-conscious about this, either. Except sometimes a person can benefit from learning to direct, or position, consciousness just a bit differently. And I think you know the kind of person I mean.

Empath gifts direct the *subconscious* mind towards other people. Positioning consciousness back at yourself — at the *conscious* level — while you are awake — now that's what will keep your empath gifts turned OFF.

PART TWO

Embracing Your Empath Gifts

Brave Empath, it's so important to embrace your gifts. Not just so that you can use their full potential. Also to avoid wasting time.

Many "guru-prescribed" activities are, in fact, unnecessary, don't work, and — if you understand what *really* makes an empath tick — *can't* work. These include such busywork as:

- Protecting yourself against "Psychic vampires"
- Using thoughts, feelings, or behaviors to manage your sensitivity
- Constantly trying to "Clean up your energy field"
- Doing grueling, ongoing work on your psychological boundaries

Besides all this, Brave Empath, you may have been doing many other things to compensate for problems caused by Imported STUFF. Only you didn't know that. You just thought you were using a technique for personal development.

Very often this happens with energy healing. One example is how unskilled empaths can become dependent on using Emotional Freedom Technique, a.k.a. EFT or tapping.

What if you don't know which empath gifts you have? What if you don't yet have skills as an empath? Until you become skilled, any one of your empath gifts can make you feel bad, with totally unpredictable ups and downs all day long.

Many an unskilled empath has moved through this pattern with EFT: Initially, great results. Then tapping all day long, just for maintenance.

Sadly that isn't really maintaining results. True results require no further upkeep.

By contrast, habitual tapping could be a sign of diminishing returns. And for an empath? It could also be a sign of trying to clean up Imported STUFF. Wouldn't it be better to prevent that icky in the first place?

One chapter at a time, let's conduct a depth survey of 15 very different empath gifts. Get ready to write down your personal **LIST OF MY EMPATH GIFTS**, a list made with old-fashioned pen and paper. Alternatively, use a favorite electronic technology.

Just avoid making a list in your head. This will not work nearly as well. Trust me here, Brave Empath. Make a physical list.

In the cause of embracing your special gifts, acknowledging them on a list is the least you can do. "Embracing" implies a certain physicality, or where is the fun? Embracing your gifts is not optional in this Program for Empath Empowerment.

CHAPTER 5

Physical Intuition

Physical Intuition is the empath gift that informs you about what is happening with another person's body.

Using that gift on purpose, employing a technique for Skilled Empath Merge, an empath experiences directly what is happening with other person's physical body.

Here comes a useful term for us to start using for "The person at the receiving end of a Skilled Empath Merge." Brave Empath, let's start calling this a "**Discovery Person.**"Physical Intuition informs you about everyday human things about your Discovery Person, physical things like:

- Mia feels peppy, agreeably over-caffeinated.
- Alyssa has a different kind of vigor, more healthy and strong and in the prime of life.
- Julian looks to be about 40 years old. What a great example he is that "Sixty can be the new 40." Physically he feels in the prime of life.
- Alex feels way older than his physical age. Although his driver's license might document a chronological age of 25, there is a stiffness to his posture and movements. Somehow you tell there is stiffness in Alex's joints. Physically he feels more like a "kid" of 80.
- Susan's back hurts.
- Colin has a headache.

When information like this comes to you without your asking, that's a problem. A problem that you're going to learn to solve.

CHAPTER 6

Physical Oneness

Unlike Physical Intuition, which reveals your Discovery Person's physical life at a distance, **PHYSICAL ONENESS** brings a much more personal kind of learning. With this empath gift, sensations within your own body can change temporarily, a result of flying in spirit.

These sensations are information in physical disguise. Except what's with that, finding information about other people, displayed inside *your* body? Do you think that might complicate your life just a bit? And yet your potential for knowledge and service can be so glorious once you have mastered this gift.

- While doing Skilled Empath Merge, you register the information.
- After your technique ends, so do any physical sensations.
- Neat and clean!

And when you're not doing a Skilled Empath Merge? With your gifts turned off, no confusing ailments that come and go. No physical overwhelm. No secret fear that you're a hypochondriac. No drip-drip-drip.

CHAPTER 7

Emotional Intuition

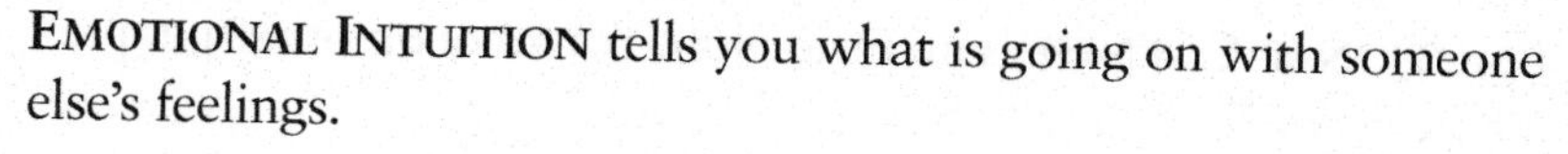

Emotional Intuition tells you what is going on with someone else's feelings.

Admittedly some non-empaths are great at *reading* emotions; same for empaths without Emotional Intuition. Anyone can develop emotional intelligence. The empath gift is different. If you can do it, you've always done it. Pretty much nonstop.

It might be nice to be with other people and *not* pay attention to what they are really feeling. But before you develop the habit of empath gifts OFF, anything can start you journeying:

- Tone of voice
- Speed of words
- Odors around the body
- Subtle variations in the person's facial skin tone

To stop the TMI overwhelm, your most productive approach is learning to turn that gift OFF, with techniques that involve consciousness.

Positioning an empath's awareness appropriately is what brings the greatest comfort. Avoid analyzing patterns of behavior... to manage distress... resulting from unskilled empath merges.

Knowing that help is on the way, you can relax and enjoy the rest of our tour of embraceable empath gifts.

CHAPTER 8

Emotional Oneness

Emotional Oneness is an inside job. You take on other people's emotions as though they belonged to you.

Maybe you're often "malled" like Emily, who thought she just hated shopping. Perhaps you wonder if you have the wrong set of friends. Or you try avoiding negative people as if they were toxic.

When moods go up and down for no apparent reason — that's awful. To some degree, *every* empath gift causes that. Which is why another term for "Unskilled empath" could be "Living in hell." Only the ups and downs happen more often with this particular empath gift.

To me, what's the weirdest part of Emotional Oneness, unskilled? The *emotional confusion.*

Most folks, empaths or not, have intense feelings. Coping with them is hard enough when all of them belong to you.

By contrast, once you develop the habit of turning your empath gifts OFF, your emotional life can become so much easier. Automatically your sense of self will grow stronger.

CHAPTER 9

Intellectual Empath Ability

Intellectual Empath Ability means a talent for energetically sharing another person's thought process.

While with others, your usual way of thinking can change so drastically, it might temporarily seem as though another person's perspective is really your own.

Are you literally thinking that other person's thoughts, like mind reading? No, it's more that you experience the other person's thinking *process*.

Which is plenty. Can that ever be confusing, at least until you become a skilled empath!

CHAPTER 10

Animal Empath Talent

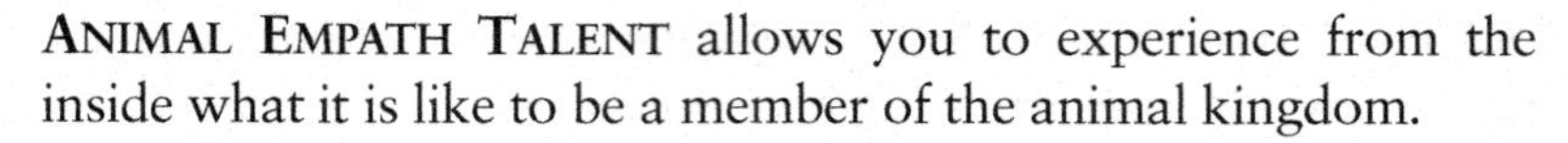

ANIMAL EMPATH TALENT allows you to experience from the inside what it is like to be a member of the animal kingdom.

Without being taught how, you learn from your pet. You can learn different ways to be. That relationship with a dog or cat or turtle can become an inspiration, a love like no other.

As a skilled empath, you can learn so much about animals, and learn it safely. Before then:

- A pet's needs can seem to trump yours
- Energetically, you can be deeply upset by the strays
- Imported STUFF can cause you to suffer along with neglected animals — and without helping them, either.
- Anger related to an animal's owners can embitter you about people, slowing you down on your path in life.
- This Imported STUFF can make you miserable, and for what? Your suffering will help neither the people who mistreat their pets nor those pets.

If you have Animal Empath Talent, it's so important to become skilled. Then, if you choose, you can become a more effective advocate for animals. In any case, you can get your life back.

CHAPTER 11

Plant Empath Talent

Some avid gardeners have it. And farmers. Sometimes it's great cooks. Also possible? You can barely make packaged ramen noodles, and right now you cultivate zero houseplants; nonetheless you could have **PLANT EMPATH TALENT**.

If you possess this magnificent empath gift, you can have it exclusively with one type of growing thing, like basil or roses. Or maybe you have it with every plant on this gorgeous green earth.

Either way, Plant Empath Talent allows you to join in consciousness with things that grow. Through consciousness, you enter into their slowly throbbing bodies and feel your human equivalent of what it is like to be them. Great, once you're doing Skilled Empath Merge.

Before then? Subconsciously, and maybe even consciously, you can hear the wails and screams... even shrieks... coming from a mostly hidden houseplant, stuck in some faraway corner, having a near-death experience... and not the nice kind, either.

If you can relate to Plant Empath Talent, this alone could explain a lot of suffering that has happened — for no reason that crossed your mind consciously — a subconscious and energetic problem caused by Imported STUFF.

A problem caused by empath gifts habitually turned ON.

Well, that's about to change.

CHAPTER 12

Crystal Empath Talent

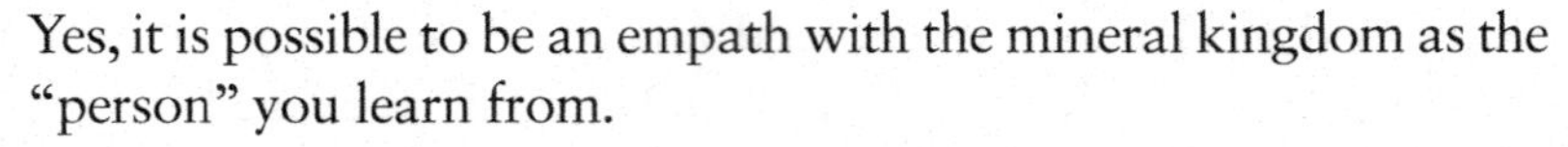

Yes, it is possible to be an empath with the mineral kingdom as the "person" you learn from.

CRYSTAL EMPATH TALENT allows you to experience directly what it is like to be an aquamarine or a diamond, some wise old rock by a river bed or, perhaps, a splendid pebble that empaths with different gifts might overlook in the woods.

Yet many a born empath with this wonderful gift might overlook the suffering it causes, picking up random Imported STUFF. Because crystals store their owner's pain energetically.

This can become your problem until your empath gifts are habitually turned OFF.

In preparation for when you become a Master Empath, you can start now to save photos from the Oscars and similar gatherings, where much-photographed stars are wearing priceless gems. Or visit museums that display legendary gems, such as The Hope Diamond, often photographed, and on display for free at the Smithsonian Institution in Washington, D.C.

Because later you can learn to do Skilled Empath Merge with these treasures. Or with your own personal gemstones and jewelry. A celestial delight!

CHAPTER 13

Environmental Empath Talent

What if you were born with **Environmental Empath Talent**?

Then you have a gift for linking your consciousness with the body of Mother Earth. One way to tell if you have this gift is to recall what happens while you take a walk someplace beautiful.

Exploring nature, most people see or smell or touch or taste... while consciousness stays right on the surface. Travel provides us with plenty to enjoy. But let's be clear. Swapping around your environment does not necessarily mean the same thing as making a shift to your consciousness.

For that, a person needs Environmental Empath Talent.

Before you gain skills, what's the problem? When a glade of trees near you is cut down to make way for yet another shopping center, it can hurt. Likewise, you may suffer due to destruction of rainforests on another continent entirely.

Far-fetched? Not really.

All on earth are connected in consciousness. Until you get yourself skills, you will suffer needlessly, depending on how much talent you have as an Environmental Empath.

You deserve to taste nature's flavors of joy. To do this with clarity and energetic protection, just keep moving forward in this Program for Empath Empowerment.

CHAPTER 14

Mechanical Empath Talent

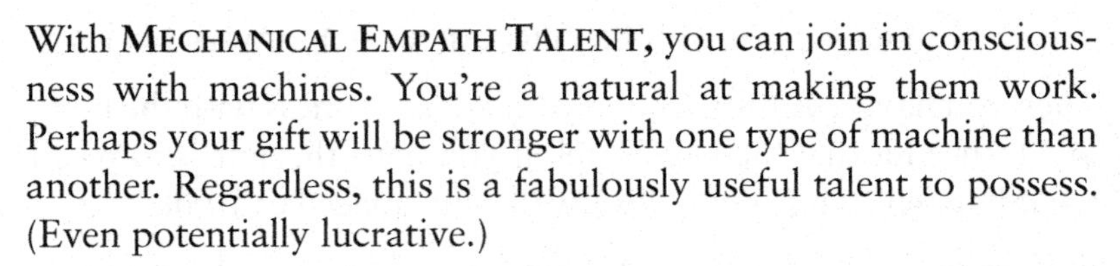

With **MECHANICAL EMPATH TALENT,** you can join in consciousness with machines. You're a natural at making them work. Perhaps your gift will be stronger with one type of machine than another. Regardless, this is a fabulously useful talent to possess. (Even potentially lucrative.)

As with other empath gifts, a Mechanical Empath isn't necessarily talented at experiencing how *all* machines operate. Your version might apply only to computers or sewing machines. The point is that you have the talent.

Each type of machine has its own consciousness, much like a farm animal. Its mechanical body has its equivalent of normal health versus illness.

Machines can develop glitches, ouches, pain. These hidden problems can become Imported STUFF in you... bringing suffering without your necessarily fixing anything in objective reality.

Imported STUFF. As if you needed that!

When you have empath skills, this particular talent becomes so worthwhile. You reclaim your life energetically, as being about you.

Beyond that, should you wish to experience more about a machine's consciousness, just do a very brief, circumscribed Skilled Empath Merge on the machine of your choice. That clean and simple.

CHAPTER 15

Medical Empath Talent

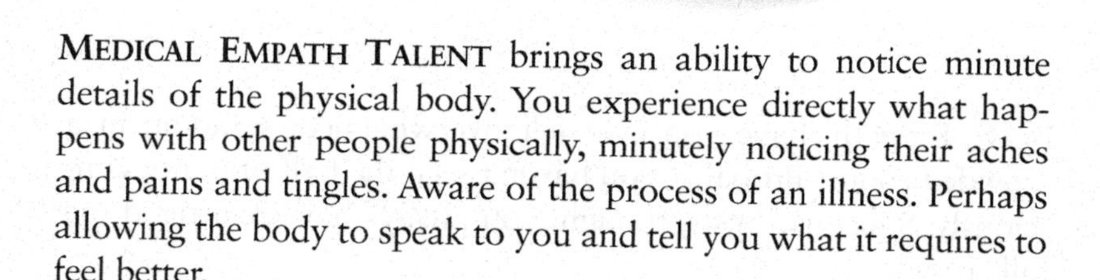

MEDICAL EMPATH TALENT brings an ability to notice minute details of the physical body. You experience directly what happens with other people physically, minutely noticing their aches and pains and tingles. Aware of the process of an illness. Perhaps allowing the body to speak to you and tell you what it requires to feel better.

This is different from being a **MEDICAL INTUITIVE**, a psychic who has trained to receive health-related information.

Medical Empaths show certain distinctive abilities in their auras:

- The specific empath gift for being a Medical Empath
- Plus Physical Intuition and/or Physical Oneness
- Plus mechanical ability
- Plus the kind of intelligence that can soak up information about how the physical body works.

Sound great? Don't envy this too much. Medical Empath Talent can make you feel like a walking emergency room.

As you may know from (very) personal experience, this empath gift can result in Imported STUFF. Just like any empath gift.

In this case, that Imported STUFF can be too disgusting to mention. In extreme cases, it has sent some unskilled empaths to the hospital for a while.

Yet when that talent is combined with empath skills, you can relax and enjoy yourself. Use your gift when you choose. Nevermore will this gift use *you*.

CHAPTER 16

Empath Talent with Astral Beings

Brave Empath, have you ever felt overwhelmed, standing in a crowded room? Probably you haven't seen the half of it, not consciously. Subconsciously, though, you always have registered the full crowd.

Angels, ghosts, and other astral beings live among us. They are especially prevalent in places like hospitals, churches, casinos, and bars.

Will you notice consciously? Maybe not.

What happens regardless, if you have **EMPATH TALENT WITH ASTRAL BEINGS?**

Only Imported STUFF.

All astral-level debris in your aura will bother you more than it bothers anyone else — including other empaths who lack this particular gift.

Hey, Brave Empath, it's a good thing you are getting yourself skills.

CHAPTER 17

Spiritual Intuition

Spiritual Intuition allows you to explore spiritual experience as it really is, no illusions — especially how other people seek contact with a Higher Power.

Long before knowing you were an empath, you may have enjoyed attending services at different houses of worship. Or singing hymns from different religions, buzzing like a honeybee to reach the sweetness of that particular path.

Witnessing this sacred love, you'll do even better as a skilled empath. Meanwhile, the downside with this gift is subconsciously taking on Imported STUFF that comes from other people's religious fears, like going to hell.

Consciously, the words you wrap around those fears may be altogether different. Every human personality has distinctive vulnerabilities related to chosen lifestyle, cherished goals, and long-term belief system.

Maybe your ultimate fears right now involve sex, money, sanity, weight, or losing favor with the folks you need most:

Then *that* is the sort of worry you'll have, due to Imported STUFF. Your own personal topics of torment.

Soon you can afford to laugh and call that old distress by its rightful name: *Just some of the silly, old drip-drip-drip.*

Empath gifts demand skills to work properly, that's all.

CHAPTER 18

Molecular Empath Ability

MOLECULAR EMPATH ABILITY means that the very substance of your aura consists of superfine energies which blend easily into the auras of others at an equally superfine level.

Therefore, whenever you do an empath merge, skilled or unskilled, you will experience your Discovery Person at a deeper level than happens with any other empath gifts.

What do you win?

Exceptional ability to validate the experiences of others. A Molecular Empath will often describe profound things to friends, describing truth at a level that they cannot consciously access or express. What a great opportunity for service to others!

Unfortunately all the Imported STUFF you take on will be extra intense, too.

The process of becoming skilled is the same for you as for any other empath. You simply need those skills more.

CHAPTER 19

Spiritual Oneness

Spiritual Intuition was considered a couple of chapters ago. Maybe you can guess what is different with **SPIRITUAL ONENESS.**

A funny little disguise occurs. That other person's spiritual experience seems to belong to *you*.

Service, through Skilled Empath Merge, is just superb. Otherwise, what about Imported STUFF?

As with Spiritual Intuition, you can internalize other people's religious or spiritual fears, labeling them in terms that seem completely unrelated, like worrying about weight or marital status. That's the content, the bits of subconscious grumbling that reach your conscious awareness.

Well, these fears can turn extra sneaky with Spiritual Oneness. Because you experience the exact *quality* of that particular fear while, weirdly, you feel like it's coming from you. So self-doubt turns even more intense.

In the past, you may never have considered that so many worries of yours really belonged to other people. With this Program for Empath Empowerment, you can experience a new clarity.

Empath gifts OFF. Yes, OFF.

This can bring a new ease, and grace, and flow, to everyday life.

CHAPTER 20

The List of My Empath Gifts, Completed

Now that you've put your list together, take one more look.

Was it one empath gift or many?

Either way, you're still an empath.

No Giving Yourself a Hard Time!

Do some empath gifts seem like more of a big deal than others?

With all respect, that doesn't matter. When you have skills, they turn all your gifts OFF. Not just your current faves. Nor the ones that seem most important. All of your empath gifts will turn OFF.

So what was the purpose of going through all this list-making? To help you gain important self-knowledge.

- Doesn't your past make more sense now?
- Do certain kinds of suffering, especially, make more sense?
- Have you gained a new context for ways you used to blame yourself, perhaps?

Developing this personal context for "empath" will help you to notice when results come your way. Because when that *drip-drip-drip* stops, those results will be deeply personal and very human.

Empath Empowerment isn't some kind of "One-size-fits-all. Zap, suddenly you're perfect!" Still, it is possible to generalize in some ways about empath gifts, like how they work. What happens, exactly, during unskilled empath merge? You're about to find out.

PART THREE

How Your Embraceable Gifts Really Work

Brave Empath, eventually you will be so grateful for every one of your God-given gifts as an empath. Although each gift is unique, every one of them works in the same manner. Here are the basic facts of life for an empath.

- Each empath gift is given to you for life.
- It comes to you switched ON.
- Until you get skills, automatically, you will do countless unskilled empath merges each day. Drip-drip-drip!
- Sometimes this flying in spirit is semi-conscious and feels good. Still it's an unskilled empath merge.
- Most of your unskilled empath merges happen subconsciously only. Your conscious mind doesn't feel or notice a thing.
- Either way, every unskilled empath merge deposits Imported STUFF in your energy field (a.k.a. Your aura).
- It can become a habit, keeping your empath gifts automatically turned OFF. No more drips, just a wonderful faucet that you can control.
- Whenever you choose, you can purposely turn your empath gifts ON. Do this safely by using a technique for Skilled Empath Merge.

Now that you have begun to embrace all your empath gifts, you're ready to understand more about how they work. Here is what you will learn in Part Three:

- What energy dynamics, exactly, occur during unskilled empath merge?
- How can you prevent this from happening?
- Why will it be effortless for you to control all your empath gifts?

CHAPTER 21

How Empath Merges Work

To fly in spirit feels so freeing. And when you can do this through Skilled Empath Merge, that sense of liberation will be yours to use at will, no strings attached.

Before then, unfortunately, you may do plenty of unskilled empath merges. Even if you have no clue they are happening. Even if they do not feel as if you are doing something wonderful, with a lovely name like "Flying in spirit."

How much do you know about unskilled empath merge? It took me more than a decade, working with students worldwide, to learn the secrets I'm about to share with you.

Your next step of learning, Brave Empath? Take this quiz.

EMPATH MERGE QUIZ. Test Your Knowledge

Answer TRUE or FALSE to the questions below. Then keep reading.

1. Even if you haven't developed skills yet, instinctively an empath knows how to stay safe while flying in spirit. T F
2. You can always choose whether or not to do an empath merge. T F
3. Probably you don't do many empath merges while with other people. T F
4. You would never do an empath merge with a stranger unless that person were really inspiring. T F

5.	On occasion you might do an empath merge just to lift someone's pain, help somebody out.	**T**	**F**
6.	It is Christian (or otherwise spiritually virtuous) to give someone the gift of an empath merge.	**T**	**F**
7.	If God gave you talent as an empath, you are obliged to use it for flying in spirit.	**T**	**F**
8.	If you feel bad after doing an empath merge, it's because you healed that person.	**T**	**F**
9.	Could be, one major reason friends love you is how you give to them as an empath.	**T**	**F**
10.	Unless you feel it happening, you are not doing an empath merge.	**T**	**F**

Expand Your Knowledge

Sure, we'll get to the answers to this "Test Your Knowledge" Quiz. Think about them for a while first.

Unconventional as a way to proceed? Sure. But I'm teaching you something unconventional, and you're embracing something unconventional as well. Just the process of answering the quiz questions could have stirred up some confusing assumptions within you, Brave Empath — conscious ideas and also maybe some subconscious expectations. Both have to go.

Let's clear the way for understanding that aligns with energetic truth, bringing words to experiences that you may never have considered before. Aligning with the truth about empath merge will prepare you to manage your empath gifts as nothing else can.

Information that follows comes from doing thousands of sessions of Rosetree Energy Spirituality, researching auras all the way through to chakra databanks, and teaching Empath Empowerment to clients all over the world.

What Happens with Unskilled Empath Merge

During an UNSKILLED EMPATH MERGE, the empath's aura expands to encompass another person's aura. I'll use the example of empath Isabella and her friend Sigmund.

It's as though Isabella gives Sigmund a hug with her energy field. This is an *energy hug*, random and entirely subconscious. More like a reflex than hugging on purpose.

Unskilled empath merge happens without conscious intent, like when a doctor smacks beneath your knee to check a physical reflex, causing your leg to jerk.

What happens right after Isabella energetically hugs Sigmund? Her energy field returns to normal size around her physical body.

Usually Isabella is totally unaware that she has done this. The aura-level hug happened subconsciously. Moreover, unskilled empath merges typically take way less than one second.

Nevertheless, an unskilled empath merge can sometimes takes longer. Empath Isabella might consciously notice what is happening, however vaguely. She might have a familiar warm-fuzzy feeling, or sense a pleasant kind of spiritual upliftment.

This would be a PROLONGED UNSKILLED EMPATH MERGE, lasting for several seconds or, even, minutes. Some unskilled empaths develop the habit of doing them routinely.

In duration, this is the opposite of most unskilled empath merges. I like to call them SPLIT-SPLIT-SECOND EMPATH MERGES for short. (The longer name would be "Split-split-split-split-split-split-split-split-split-split-split-split- split-split-split-split- split-split-split-split- split-split-split-split-second empath merges.) (Approximately.)

Split-Split-Second Empath Merges happen way too fast for conscious detection.

Will this brevity somehow protect an empath from suffering the consequences? Nope.

Regardless of duration, each unskilled empath merge results in Imported STUFF for the empath.

Does Prolonged Unskilled Empath Merge deposit more than the super-quick varieties? Probably.

All the more reason to detect it, stop it and, over time, prevent it completely.

CHAPTER 22

More About Prolonged Unskilled Empath Merges

Split-Split-Second Empath Merges don't show to a casual observer. But Prolonged Unskilled Empath Merges do, at least to a trained observer.

Vision patterns can provide a clue. For instance, what if you see Isabella staring for a long period of time at Sigmund? What if she is staring almost like a baby, with rapt attention? What's happening might be a Prolonged Unskilled Empath Merge.

More complication, though! Isabella might just like Sigmund's tie. Or Isabella might be stoned on weed. Only aura reading would definitively reveal what is happening with Isabella's consciousness.

When an unskilled empath merge is prolonged, would Isabella necessarily know what she's doing? Does she sense how her auric field expands to encompass Sigmund's energy field, akin to blowing up a large balloon that surrounds another balloon? Probably not.

More likely, if Isabella verbalized her mostly subconscious, warm fuzzy feeling, she would call it: "I really love him." Or "Losing myself in Sigmund is what it means to be a really good friend."

Unless Isabella has studied with Obi Wan Kenobi (or the equivalent), she will not consciously notice random fluctuations in energy fields, a.k.a., "The Force." That would be a good thing, actually. Outside a "Star Wars" movie, it isn't particularly healthy to dwell on auras all day long. Even the spiritually Enlightened do not do this. Reading auras all day long leads to spiritual addiction, which you can learn about at my blog and some of my other books.

After Unskilled Empath Merge What Changes?

Once Isabella's aura reverts to its usual dimensions, she returns to her normal sense of self — for the moment. Until her next unskilled empath merge, which could happen any second.

Even then, there's a tricky after-effect. It happens after every single unskilled empath merge. "Returning to normal" means returning to a slightly different form of normal. Because some of the Imported STUFF in Sigmund's aura has transferred to Isabella's own energy field. Where that STUFF becomes her personal problem, long term.

Temporarily, Sigmund feels better subconsciously. He might even feel better consciously. Why wouldn't he? Here is what happens in one hypothetical example of Split-Split-Second Empath Merge. When some of Sigmund's psychic-level STUFF has just been transferred to Isabella, that includes:

- 25 blobs of psychic coercion, each one related to feeling sexually inadequate
- 15 small frozen blocks fraught with anxiety
- 12 negative thought forms contributing to low self-esteem

All of these globs and blobs and blocks of stuck, negative energy are now Isabella's problem. Remain in her aura they will... until she receives depth energy healing.

Sadly, Sigmund's relief is temporary. He has received an energy clearing, not a true healing. There has been no PUT-IN, neither energetically nor in terms of a meaningful conscious Aha!

So Isabella has paid a pretty steep price for brief glimpses of Otherness, hasn't she?

Although this example is hypothetical, I have helped real-life clients to remove exactly the sorts of STUFF described here. For years, the presence of all this STUFF flabbergasted me. How could certain clients carry so much random astral debris? Then I figured out the common denominator. All those clients were unskilled empaths.

If this hidden side of being an empath disturbs you, good. Now you know why I urge all my clients and students to make empath skills a priority in their personal development (assuming that they are empaths in the first place).

As a teacher, I offer instruction in many useful skill sets for aura healing and deeper perception. Yet whenever an empath asks me, "Where do you recommend that I start?" my answer is simple. I will urge that empath to gain Empath Empowerment.

Many an empath is bent way out of shape energetically, due to volunteer work like Isabella's unskilled merge with Sigmund, leaving her aura stuck with those dismal energy souvenirs.

Randomly picking up Imported STUFF is unavoidable... until that empath learns how to support inborn talent with skill, and routinely keep empath gifts OFF. Incidentally, you may be wondering about those empath talents *not* related to human beings.

By now you appreciate that unskilled empath merges occur when an empath like Isabella is in the room with another person. What if you have one of those empath gifts not-about-humans, like Animal Empath Ability or Crystal Empath Ability?

Then you busily do volunteer work with animals or crystals. These are human-frequency objects, having a form in objective reality, and with energy fields as well. Of course, they can contain energetic STUFF.

Hello! That STUFF can, and will, move directly into your aura. With skill, Brave Empath, you will simply enjoy your consensual wisdom downloads. Managing your special gifts as an empath? Definitely that means taking on wisdom, not Imported STUFF.

CHAPTER 23

What Happens During Skilled Empath Merge?

What a refreshing contrast, to consider something empath that's voluntary and healthy!

Nobody slip-slides into Skilled Empath Merge. This requires choice. You select one technique you have learned. Then you do it purposely. Afterwards you consciously stop doing the technique.

Thus, each short-term voyage in consciousness is structured to have a distinct beginning, middle, and end.

Imagine that, as a skilled empath, Isabella wishes to probe the consciousness of her friend Sigmund. She chooses the "Deep Listening" technique (which you can learn from the follow-up book in this series, *The Master Empath)*. She asks Sigmund for permission to learn about him from the inside, using her consciousness. After doing the technique, she will report back to him.

Let's suppose further that Sigmund agrees. Then Isabella does what she has said she would do. So inspiring, and insightful for them both! In some ways, this consensual empath merge could be better than sex: Pure consciousness pleasure, with no strings attached.

Whichever technique you select to use on any particular occasion, what will happen in general when you do a Skilled Empath Merge?

A Divine blessing will protect you.

Yes, every technique for Skilled Empath Merge will allow you to co-create with your favorite form of Highest Power. That protection is layered in many different ways. And it works.

Behold that Skilled Empath Glow

Continuing with the example of Isabella, what happens aurically during her Skilled Empath Merge? During the first few steps of "Deep Listening," her aura takes on an extra glow of Divine protection.

Once prepared, her aura encircles Sigmund's. How long does this sort of auric hug last? Isabella consciously chooses, based on what feels comfortable to her at the time. Usually the duration ranges from 10 seconds to a minute.

Not long, you'll notice, Brave Empath. Yet even the shortest Skilled Empath Merge will last significantly longer than a Split-Split-Second Unskilled Empath Merge.

Afterwards Isabella's aura returns to normal dimensions, completely separate from Sigmund's. And what changes within her energetically, resulting from this Skilled Empath Merge?

Nothing. Sigmund's STUFF remains in Sigmund. Isabella's aura remains normal, too. Even the Divine glow gradually subsides.

However, Isabella does learn something consciously:

- In terms of *content,* she learns about what it is like, right now, being Sigmund.
- In terms of *process,* she exercises her ability to consciously fly in spirit.
- *Mastery of her empath gifts* progresses as well. Mastery develops every time that Isabella uses her talent as it was meant to be used. The skill is cumulative.
- If Isabella has additional skills for helping Sigmund, her personal *efficacy* can also grow considerably.

That efficacy is a really important advantage, not just for self-esteem but for accomplishing great things in life. Supplementing her Skilled Empath Merge, Isabella may well use her friendship skills.

Definitely, that counts as **EFFICACY**, a way to be effective in life. Effectiveness earned.

Efficacy is not some lucky accident. It happens because a person has developed a skill set which is purposely used to produce a desired result.

So, after ending the Skilled Empath Merge, Isabella might apply any professional skills that she has learned, like massage therapy or giving Sigmund a great haircut or effectively cutting a cord of attachment.

All her efficacy will be enhanced, thanks to first having done that Skilled Empath Merge.

Isabella's skills will adapt in subtle ways, since she has just experienced from the inside what it is like to be this completely different person. Automatically she will apply her skills based on Sigmund's unique "Who-you-be," rather than expecting Sigmund to be "Just like me."

This will help to make Isabella's actions way more effective than otherwise. More efficacy, informed by deep knowing — that can be your destiny too, Brave Empath.

Let's note further, deep knowing like this is not a psychic experience, astrally based. Rather, Isabella has made a brief journey in consciousness to explore both Divine and astral frequencies of Sigmund's aura. That journey supports her human life, and doesn't make her seem floaty or odd.

This kind of knowing is simple, direct, and energy intensive. Nonetheless Isabella's experience has been structured in a way that supports her own humanity.

No wonder the results of a Skilled Empath Merge can help Isabella to get her life together — just the opposite of the spaced-out, energy-entangled lifestyle of an unskilled empath.

Brave Empath, beyond efficacy with your professional skill sets, Skilled Empath Merge can be combined with ordinary life skills to help you become extra successful in life, period.

This is what I mean by **BECOMING A MASTER EMPATH.** Applications abound for love, business, and friendship — bringing you a real competitive advantage. (For specifics, see *The Master Empath*. But, please, only after you have learned more about how to turn your empath gifts OFF.)

Right now, at your stage of progress in this Program for Empath Empowerment, I have a challenge for you. Brave Empath, let's return to our learning-in-progress, that Empath Merge Quiz.

Do you wish to change any of your answers before moving forward to answers supplied by Rose, your friendly empath coach? And are you prepared for surprises?

CHAPTER 24

Empath Merge Quiz. ANSWERS

Brave Empath, you deserve to know the energetic truth. Your whole life you've been doing unskilled empath merge, yet how much have you known about it?

1. ***Even if you haven't developed skills yet, instinctively an empath knows how to stay safe while flying in spirit.***

FALSE

By definition, no unskilled empath merge is safe. Sorry.

While unskilled, some empaths will suffer more than others. The *number of empath gifts* is a factor. The more gifts you have as an empath, the more you will suffer.

2. ***You can always choose whether or not to do an empath merge.***

FALSE, MOSTLY

Usually an empath has no choice whatsoever. So many unskilled empath merges happen in random fashion, done with strangers, lasting a millisecond.

Hardly what I would call "Always choosing"! Sometimes, though, even an unskilled empath has some a degree of choice.

This choice concerns whether the empath is going to stay in the merge for an extra-long period of time, longer than a split-split second. Remember our discussion of Prolonged Unskilled Empath

Merge? That can bring a sweet sense of connection, a pleasurable and familiar conscious experience related to empath merge.

Provided that you do notice this — and granted, most empaths do not — the state of connection can be prolonged intentionally. Which could become a habit, a bad habit. You might think it's soulful or sexy. Sadly, other people may not find it quite so endearing. Even if they are too polite to tell you.

---

3. ***Probably you don't do many empath merges while with other people.***

FALSE

Not do many of those merges? Says who, your conscious mind?

Remember, Brave Empath, unskilled empath merges are not performed by your conscious mind.

It's more like a reflex at aura level, comparable to muscles that work involuntarily.

With skill, it can become so effortless — and routine — to keep all your empath gifts turned OFF as a matter of habit. Then you definitely won't be doing random empath merges with others.

---

4. ***You would never do an empath merge with a stranger unless that person were really inspiring.***

FALSE

Subconsciously every human alive reads everyone else's aura. It's as if each of us were a runway model in the fashion show of life, constantly displaying our every energetic characteristic. My term for that is AURIC MODELING.

How can auric modeling can trigger unskilled empath merge?

- A stranger's aura includes certain kinds of suffering that are familiar to you, based on past experience. Subconsciously you could be drawn to this.

- Any troubled person's aura might remind you of difficult people from your past.
- A person's auric modeling is unusual... and in a way that relates to your personal set of gifts as an empath. "Look, he's got Intellectual Empath Ability. Just like me!"

Oops! You're curious, subconsciously. Well, if your empath gifts have been ON anyway, why not slip-slide into an unskilled empath merge? (Developing the habit of empath gifts OFF will protect you.)

5. ***On occasion you might do an empath merge just to lift someone's pain, help somebody out.***

TRUE, also **FALSE**

First, the TRUE part. Sure, feeling sorry for someone might trigger a Split-Split-Second Empath Merge or even a Prolonged Empath Merge.

Mostly, though, the answer to Quiz Question #5 is FALSE. Let's be clear. Does an unskilled empath ever, really "lift someone's pain"?

Not long term. Not significantly. Sorry.

Temporary relief may be felt. But that other person has not received permanent healing. Sadly, subconscious STUFF will soon return to his energy field. Meanwhile you have accumulated more imported STUFF, which becomes your problem.

6. ***It is Christian (or otherwise spiritually virtuous) to give someone the gift of an empath merge.***

TRUE, also **FALSE**

What could be more personal than your deciding what is virtuous?

One example: Does your belief system exalt sacrifice? If so, this Quiz Question #6 would count as TRUE.

Suppose that Empath Ben sees that his friend Gloria is suffering. Even if he doesn't have empath skills yet, he might sense how to do a Prolonged Unskilled Empath Merge. Further, he might consciously have figured out that he will pay a personal price, and feel terrible afterwards. Yet, out of duty — or his love of God — Ben might do plenty of Prolonged Unskilled Empath Merges, simply in order to be a good friend.

As a conscious rationale Ben's choice might go, "If I can make Gloria feel better, even for a few moments, what does it matter if I must pay for it afterwards?"

Of course, a rationale like that could also be called "Co-dependency." A lovely religious faith can be mixed in with co-dependency, like pearls in the mud.

Brave Empath, after you have become a skilled empath, you can help a friend like Gloria without suffering as a result. You can help her better. Which is why, personally, my answer to Quiz Question #6 is FALSE.

Regarding your religious and ethical values, Brave Empath, here's a suggestion. After you have lived for several months as a skilled empath, sit for an hour and write a list of your current beliefs. With a freshly cleaned-up aura, not perpetually picking up STUFF from others, some of your values might change. You may choose less human sacrifice, more joy for yourself, and far more effectiveness as a helper to others.

7. ***If God gave you talent as an empath, you are obliged to use it for flying in spirit.***

FALSE

You might not agree with me about this Quiz Answer, Brave Empath. And that's fine. Because your self-authority rules, right? Besides, you are going to learn how to fly in spirit with Skilled

Empath Merge, which will be a safe way to use that lifelong empath talent.

That said, here is what I think about Quiz Question #7... and I have thought about it a lot.

Seems to me, the only way God can give anyone talent as an empath is to have it installed from Day One. (Some human gifts are just like that, although most are not.)

Learning how to develop skill to support empath talent? That part is up to us. If you do believe strongly in God, maybe you agree with one of my favorite sayings, "Heaven helps those who help themselves."

God made you an empath, but only you can make yourself a skilled empath. That's just how it is.

This Program for Empath Empowerment encourages you to use self-authority to uphold your values, deciding for yourself what is truly virtuous.

8. ***If you feel bad after doing an empath merge, it's because you healed that person.***

FALSE

Temporarily that other person might feel better. So you might have answered, TRUE, Brave Empath.

But really! Does a brief feel-good moment really count as healing someone? Fact is, neither unskilled empaths nor skilled empaths really heal people. Energy healing requires a dedicated skill set. For healing.

Seems to me, the skill set of Empath Empowerment comes as close to *self-healing* as you can get, but really that's prevention. Learning to habitually turn your empath gifts OFF will prevent your taking on STUFF from others. This could be considered a way to prevent Imported STUFF, greatly decreasing your need to receive healing.

That's as close as empath talent will get you to energy healing... for yourself or others.

9. Could be, one major reason friends love you is how you give to them as an empath.

TRUE, also **FALSE**

Sure. Who doesn't like to get something for nothing? It's human nature.

Totally TRUE, then. Your volunteer work as an unskilled empath could be a major factor in some of your friendships right now.

FALSE is a better answer, however. By the time you move into the lifestyle of a skilled empath, some so-called "Friends" may abandon you. They will gravitate towards new "Friends" who are unskilled empaths and, therefore, provide the same sort of subconscious freebie.

How about the friends who remain? Count them as real friends, the ones worth keeping.

10. Unless you feel it happening, you are not doing an empath merge.

FALSE

Brave Empath, did you laugh while answering?

By now, you know a great deal about the hidden, subconscious mechanics — the incessant volunteer work — in the life of every unskilled empath. You can afford to laugh, especially if you have started to recognize the full extent of this problem.

It is very personal, the chronic suffering of an unskilled empath. Typically, though, we blame ourselves. Even if we have never heard the word "Empath."

Feeling bad, due to all that astral-level STUFF, we can call ourselves plenty of names, worrying that we are oh-so-delicate, even dysfunctional. Really, you are not to blame for those unskilled empath merges. Other people are not to blame, either. Blame the process itself, Brave Empath. Then learn how to stop it.

Sure you can. You are in a Program for Empath Empowerment. Where you happen to be doing just fine.

CHAPTER 25

Ten Reasons Why Something So Bad Feels So Good

Flying in spirit usually causes an empath to feel liberated. Even if later you'll suffer due to Imported STUFF. Here I'll use the example of doing unskilled empath merge with Joe. Why can something so bad for you... feel so good?

1. You have moved out of the box of your consciousness into the box of Joe's consciousness. Such variety! It adds spice to life.
2. If your experience was *unpleasant*, at least it was temporary. Back at your own experience, you can feel better by comparison. Returning to your everyday sense of self, your consciousness positioned comfortably back at normal subjective reality, it's as though you just took an exotic vacation.
3. If the experience happened to be *pleasant*, you gained inspiration. Like viewing a lovely painting at the art museum.
4. While flying in spirit, you might feel caring. As an unskilled empath, you might even label your passing mood as "My friend Joe really needs me."
5. After the empath merge, you may sense that you have helped Joe, just because some of his subconscious STUFF has moved out for 10 minutes. (Of course, long-term, nothing will change for Joe. Another version of his old STUFF will return soon.)

6. Flying in spirit feels natural to you, having been done so easily. By comparison, so much else in life is hard. Even counting from 1-10 takes more effort.

Now, Brave Empath, please don't be offended at the remaining four reasons on this list. Keep in mind, flying in spirit is very different for an unskilled empath compared to how it will be after you have learned how to keep your gifts OFF.

7. Flying in spirit may *feel* spiritual, as if you are doing something that brings you closer to the Divine. In a way that is true, but in a way that is not true at all. (Until you have lived for a while as a very skilled empath, this difference may be hard to believe. For now, just keep your mind open to the possibility.)
8. Sense of identity for an unskilled empath might be a bit vague or confused. Borrowing Joe's sense of identity, even for that split second, could make you feel more whole as a person.
9. Before you become a skilled empath, you might also identify more with the *process* of flying in spirit than with simply being yourself. This can feel very limiting to an empath, since we are capable of readily sampling such different human experiences.
10. It's fun. Variety keeps away the dreaded, common experience of same old, same old. Other things being equal would you rather have 20 meals a day, 20 "Favorite" foods, maybe even 20 faithful lovers, and at least 20 cats? Seriously, Brave Empath, all of us want to be more, to have more. That's not greed necessarily, just human nature. Well, flying in spirit allows you to sample consciousness.

Safe sampling will become way more fun later, when you do only Skilled Empath Merge. Actually, regular everyday life for a skilled empath can also become huge fun... long before you start doing Skilled Empath Merge.

The techniques you're about to learn in Part Four will start you *managing* your special empath gifts. Managing means ending the drip-drip-drip. Can you imagine what it will like to spend your waking hours without the confusions of subconscious Imported STUFF?

Once you start turning your empath gifts OFF, that will automatically turn ON something else. Something distinctive, fresh and fascinating, even sacred. Your sense of self.

PART FOUR

Manage Your Magnificent Empath Gifts

If you need to blame someone, blame God.

Even almighty God might have some limitations. Because it appears that the only way God can bestow any empath gift is for it to be installed in the turned-ON position.

Actually, I don't blame God. I love God. And it really doesn't need to be anyone's fault why, on this Learning Planet, certain things work as they do.

The sky will always point upwards, for instance. At least when you stand on the ground and look up.

Why fight the system when that same energy could be applied to *working* the system?

So what if empath gifts are installed in the turned-ON position? No repining! Right now, Brave Empath, you can learn skills to purposely turn those gifts OFF. This will protect you from picking up STUFF from random, unskilled empath merges.

Let's start exploring how to turn your empath gifts OFF.

That begins with an unexpected upgrade, improving something you might not have thought needed improvement at all.

CHAPTER 26

How to Gently Manage Consciousness

What follows is a simple technique to help you manage your flow of consciousness. After you try it, keep reading and then (as you will be doing with every technique that follows in this book) join my virtual classroom for a session of Questions & Answers.

Brave Empath, keep reading about this technique *only* when prepared to take the 5-10 minutes you'll need to actually do it. Otherwise skip ahead to the next chapter.

Notice, Brave Empath, this is your recommended strategy for every technique presented henceforth in our Program for Empath Empowerment. Either commit to actually doing the technique or skip it completely, for now.

For Best Results with Any Technique Here

Here is all you need do:

- Make reasonably sure that you will not be interrupted. Turn off electronic gizmos. Alert your roommates. Fling pets from the room. (Okay, Gentle Empath, you might prefer gently carrying Fido out of the room. Definitely close the door afterwards.)
- Sit comfortably, feet on the ground or supported by a good, sturdy pillow.
- Avoid chewing gum. Or tobacco. Or cookies. Or other food, drink, cigarettes, etc.
- Read through all the technique steps in advance.

- While techniquing, open your eyes to peek at those steps again, as needed. Close your eyes quickly after each peek and you will be doing just fine.
- What about fretting over "Supposed to"? As in, "How am I supposed to feel while doing this?" Fugeddaboutit. Just do the steps, Brave Empath. Afterwards see the Q&A.

Technique: HEY, YOU

Who are you, really? What does it mean to become conscious of your consciousness?

Brave Empath, do the following steps nice and sloppy and easy. Then proceed immediately to the Q&A section that follows.

- Beginning this effortless technique, sit comfortably and close your eyes. This will automatically *direct your attention within.*
- To bring a bit more clarity to your experience, *take a few deep breaths.* Sit there for a while. Then ask yourself this question: *"What do I notice?"* It could be thoughts, emotions, physical sensations, energy, images, silence, whatever — in any combo. Continue gently noticing whatever you spontaneously notice, not trying to make anything happen.
- After about one minute, put names to the *type* of experience you were just having. Was it thoughts, emotions, physical sensations, energy, images, what?
- Say out loud whichever type(s) of thing you just noticed.
- Think, "Technique officially over" *Open your eyes.* Automatically this will direct your awareness outward, to objective reality.

Q&A. Hey, You

Q. *Trying to put this consciousness thing into words makes me feel stupid. Why can't I just call whatever happened "Whatever"?*

A. Languaging your experience will enhance it in the long run. Stretch yourself.

Q. *But what if all I have to say is "Boring"? Nothing amazing happened. All I got was a quiet kind of state. For all I know, I was asleep.*

A. Were you drooling on your shirt? If not, don't call it sleep.

Q. *Can you give examples of what other empaths notice when you teach them the "Hey, You" Technique?*

A. Sure. Just don't compare yourself to anyone else. Each of these is a fine answer, and there are innumerable others.

- Silence.
- A new sound of silence within ordinary silence.
- Darkness.
- Light.
- A discovery that you, the real you deep inside, are a kind of dancing light.
- Random thoughts.
- Random emotions.
- Worrying about my thoughts or emotions.
- Noticing flows of energy inside my body.
- Seeing inner images or cartoons.

Q. *So which of these experiences of consciousness is the best kind to have?*

A. Every one of them. Any one of them. Or something else entirely. What happened to you, whatever you noticed effortlessly with your consciousness. That is the best.

Q. *But what if I did work hard?*

A. That was a misunderstanding. Please go back and do the technique again. Discover how your consciousness is plenty lively all on its own, no effort needed.

CHAPTER 27

Like Yourself Better

Who is this person, you? How well do you like yourself?

Speaking English, we're fortunate to have two very separate words, love and like. Do you LOVE yourself?

Probably. That would be the unconditional kind of love, a recognition that deep down you are such a good person: Funny, fun, sweet, and all your other adorable qualities.

Soul-level qualities, they could be considered. Your familiar deep-down love for your essential goodness could be called UNCONDITIONAL LOVE. As the unique soul you are, Brave Empath, you may find it easy to love yourself.

Now for a very different question: Do you LIKE yourself?

Depends, doesn't it?

- Getting out of bed on a Sunday morning, hung over from your festivities the night before? Maybe not liking yourself totally.
- A friend says, "You're great." You think, "Hey, I really am special."
- Another friend says, "It isn't you. It's me. We must break up." You think, "Oh, it's me alright. How can I live with myself? Do I even like this person?"

Liking yourself could seem harder than loving yourself, and for good reason. You are a spiritual being having a human experience. Unconditional love for that spiritual being is simple.

But wrapping your mind and heart around your ever-changing, way-complicated, human existence?

That's **Conditional Liking.** Which is way harder. Even for non-empaths, conditional self-liking is pretty hard. Think of non-empaths you know with a sturdy sense of self. How do they pull it together?

- Consider your buddy Natalie. Her sense of comes from things that she owns: Familiar things, pretty things; jewelry with sentimental value; a gorgeous painting in her living room. When Natalie wants to feel better about herself, she goes shopping and buys something new to like. Maintaining this form of conditional liking could be hard, especially paying for all that shopping! Hard, but manageable.
- Or think of Charlie, your employee at work. His sense of self is power-related, based on comparing his status to that of others. When Charlie is one-up, he likes himself. When one-down, he doesn't like himself nearly so much. Even so, Charlie can plot and plan to win the next competition. The very fact that Charlie constantly struggles to win high status? That could be reason enough to conditionally like himself. Competing like this would be hard, but sometimes fun, and altogether quite manageable.
- How about you? Is your sense of self really so simple? Does it depend entirely on one or two outer aspects of life, like your appearance or financial status or popularity or the thrill of your sex life? Your personal sense of identity may be way more nuanced. (Which would be typical for an empath.)

Conditional liking for yourself while you are an unskilled empath? Hello, this can be nearly impossible!

- Whatever your values or interests or lifestyle, what happens due to the perpetual travel? Subconsciously you keep moving into the values or interests or lifestyle of other people. Might feel like you're always comparing yourself, yet actually be something different — the habit of unskilled empath merge.

Developing a sturdy, human sense of identity, and liking it? That's where an empath can be a later bloomer.

Besides all the subconscious experiences, confusing forms of identification result, and another factor is all the Imported STUFF. How difficult it becomes, developing a strong sense of self and coming to like that particular human identity.

Goodbye, Earthquakes

Have you ever lived through an earthquake? Even a tiny one on the Richter scale can deliver quite a shakeup.

We humans expect the earth to be stable beneath our feet. Most of the time it is, so we take that for granted.

After an earthquake, even a brief one, what automatically happens to your easy certainty? You may not be so sure. A certain kind of trust has been shaken along with the ground.

What if you were to live through an earthquake without paying much attention? Subconsciously you would still notice, correct? Subconsciously, a certain kind of trust would be shaken along with the ground. Well, moving in consciousness into another person's energy field produces something like that. The subconscious shift in identity can destabilize your sense of self.

No, the physical ground beneath your feet does not give way. However, your everyday sense of being "Me-Me-Me" shifts over to "What Is Happening to Somebody Else." Temporarily, the standard human experience of "Me-Me-Me" is disrupted. Conditional liking for yourself is shaken.

Well, this is about to change for good, Brave Empath. Let's start to build up a stronger sense of yourself in very human ways."

Technique: I LIKE

Time to learn more about what your human identity happens to like. Right now!

Whether you call it *taste* or *personal preferences*, whatever you like really does matter. Back when you were two years old, you had strong personal preferences. And you have them now. (Or else you can reinstall them.)

Allowing yourself to like what you already happen to like... can intensify a health respect for Me-Me-Me.

Brave Empath, please know that personal preferences are permitted in life. Contrary to what you may have been told, good people do not blandly feel an identical liking for everyone and everything. Personal likes and dislikes are healthy.

The "I Like" technique invites you to explore your preferences for material objects. By recognizing some things that you personally like, indirectly you will strengthen your ability to like *yourself*... and trust your own first thought or feeling.

- Sit or stand somewhere you can be alone, or at least uninterrupted, for a minute or two. (Actually, this technique is excellent for times like being stuck in a long line at the supermarket, provided that you do the following steps discretely.)
- Look at your surroundings. Find a color you like a lot. Is it the blue upholstery on your chair? The bright pink lettering on a poster? A fascinating and colorful food stain on your shirt? Go for likability, pure and simple. Say why you like it out loud. "I like the color of the _____ because _____."
- Now it's sound time. Close your eyes. Such a variety of sounds is audible wherever you are. Listen and then ask yourself, "What is a sound I like, here and now?" Choose a favorite. Open your eyes and say why you like it out loud, "I like the sound of ____ because ____."

- For the final round, close your eyes again. Seek out and touch different textures, such as the fabric of your clothing, the surface of the furniture near you. Take a couple of fingers and explore your near environment until you *find a texture that especially delights you.* Open your eyes and *say why you like it* out loud, "I like the way ____ feels because ____."
- Think, "Technique over." Because it is. Open your eyes.

Q&A. I Like

Q. *That was fun, I suppose. But what did it mean?*

A. Doing the "I Like" technique did something important for Empath Empowerment. Temporarily you just turned all your empath gifts OFF.

That's because you were consciously paying attention to yourself, just yourself, that delightful human self with excellent taste.

Q. *How could I possibly do this technique in public?*

A. To avoid feeling self-conscious about being seen talking to yourself in public, pull out your smartphone and pretend to be having a conversation, sometimes listening and sometimes talking.

Q. *What about the touching part?*

A. People fidget all the time. Just touch your sleeve, your hand, some of the merchandise in your shopping cart. You can find a way to do this technique and make it socially acceptable.

Q. *It was hard for me to do this exercise. Why?*

A. "I Like" is a technique of pure selfishness and sensuality. You cease looking out for other people. Instead you jump into your own here and now. Of course, that can be hard in the beginning.

Q. *What if I keep thinking, "Who cares what I like? What does it matter?"*

A. It thrills your soul to find pleasure through your senses. That is true for any human being, empath or not.

If you have ever hungered for closer contact with your soul, guess what? It honors your soul to pay attention to what you, personally, like. So ignore any inner grumbles and keep on exploring.

Q. *Why? What did I just give my soul, supposedly?*

A. Beyond giving yourself a vacation *from* empath talent, you were giving *to* yourself. You reminded yourself that, at will, you can delight in your senses. Ask your Inner Child how it likes this technique. Because probably it's jumping for joy.

Q. *How often would you recommend playing the "I Like" game?*

A. Do it three times a day for a week, minimum. You're right, it *is* a game. And the more often you play it (within reason), the more you will enjoy it.

Q. *What is the purpose of the "because" part of the game? Why isn't it enough to choose something I like?*

A. When you push yourself a bit to say out loud why you like something, you're challenged in several ways, all beneficial.

- You stay right on the surface of life, positioning consciousness at subjective human reality. For empath skills, that's good to do.
- Probing for words can strengthen your natural ability to speak up for yourself.
- Reasons you say aloud may sound very simple, such as "I like the purple color of my calendar because it makes me feel happy." Speaking with such simplicity is good practice for you. "Because it makes me feel happy" is plenty.

As an adult, you can definitely do this. From childhood, many of us have been trained to make ourselves sound grown-up, educated, complex, sophisticated, important, logical. Yet often our personal preferences *are* childlike.

Q. *What if talking that way makes you feel uncomfortable? That's what happened to me.*

A. After you say your answers out loud, you gain a chance to practice non-judgment. *"I like the carpet because it's soft."* Maybe that's not fancy. Well if it is true for you right now, then it's true. That simple.

"*The sound of the wind in the trees feels dark brown and soothes my forehead.*" Whatever words come out of your mouth, strive to accept them without criticism.

Being human, you do like some things and dislike others, prefer some colors over others, enjoy certain foods more than others. Even true for a saint! It is so good for any empath, accepting your humanity.

Q. *I happen to have a major challenge about making decisions. This sounds stupid, but what if it takes me a really long time to choose anything to like?*

A. Keep at it. Eventually you may also improve your trust at decision-making, especially if you add one simple rule: When you're hunting for a color, sound, or texture, say your very first thought.

And here's another workaround: Set a timer for one minute. Not to pressure yourself. Just a reminder yourself to avoid drifting off into some familiar process of giving yourself a hard time.

With practice you will find it easy to just choose something before that timer goes off. Oooh, commitment! When that timer goes off, blurt something out, however ridiculous.

Finally it may help to remember that this technique can be light-hearted and fun. You're not on the witness stand in some murder trial. Pick something. Anything. With practice you just might lighten up enough to really enjoy "I Like"

Q. *What if I don't happen to have any strong likes or dislikes?*

A. Deep down you must. Watch any two-year old. Once upon a time, you were that willful. Until somebody taught you to be oh-so-polite. Well, phooey on that-ey!

"I Like" will start your spontaneity flowing. So will our next technique.

CHAPTER 28

Breathe Yourself More Awake

Brave Empath, now we will begin to explore a series of easy techniques that involve breathing. Each one makes you more resourceful for managing your special empath gifts.

Just so you know, another reason to learn all these skills is that some will serve as preparation for the "Coming Home" technique in a later chapter. Mastering that big technique requires that you learn several smaller ones first.

Meanwhile, got your nose? Got consciousness, Brave Empath? How about a bit of time? That's all you need and then you're good to go.

Breath Holding During Unskilled Empath Merge

Routine breathing can actually help you, sometimes, to turn empath gifts OFF.

Remember our previous discussion of Prolonged Unskilled Empath Merge? I noted that some of you Brave Empaths may have fallen into a habit of staring at the person with whom you were doing a semi-conscious, unskilled empath merge.

Very likely, at such times, you were also holding your breath.

Technique: INSTALL AN AUTOMATIC SUBCONSCIOUS ALERT

I'm going to help you bring in help from your subconscious mind to break the habit of slipping into Prolonged Unskilled Empath Merge.

This will provide a bit of subconscious programming for your mind-body-spirit system, helping your inner self to change something that ordinarily would not be noticed consciously.

Just read the following paragraphs silently once, and then out loud three times in a row.

First, from the waking state of consciousness, I am now speaking to the part of my subconscious mind responsible for breathing. From now on, while I am awake, if I start holding my breath as part of an unskilled empath merge, please alert me.

Second, from the waking state of consciousness, I am now speaking to the part of my subconscious mind responsible for blinking my eyes. From now on, while I am awake, please alert me if I start staring at someone or something as part of an unskilled empath merge.

What does that mean, "Alert me"? Subconscious mind, send me a quick thought or feeling, in a gentle way, that is instantly noticeable to my conscious mind. This instant inner message will go like this: "You have started doing unskilled empath merge. Come back to reality. Now."

This alert is comparable to inner notifications that I have already established for myself, like knowing when I need to use the toilet. A subconscious inner alert of this kind is no big deal, yet clear enough for my conscious mind to get the message.

Once I receive the conscious message, it will be easy for me to resume regular breathing in and out. Automatically I will begin to pay attention in the here and now, whatever interests me in objective reality.

This new mechanism for self-awareness requires no effort from my conscious mind. Once installed, it works automatically. I install this mechanism now.

Q&A. Install an Automatic Subconscious Alert

Q. *Hold on. Are you suggesting that I monitor my blinking and breathing all day long?*

A. Please, no. Becoming self-conscious like that would amount to a cure that is worse than the disease.

Actually, monitoring yourself all day long — about blinking or anything else — is a "cure" that would *worsen* the disease.

When skilled, an empath lives naturally. Not in a state of perpetual self-consciousness.

This one-time technique simply activates the power of your subconscious mind to give you spontaneous feedback. In our Program for Empath Empowerment, this is one of many techniques for turning empath gifts OFF.

Q. *I'm a scientist with strong interest in brain functioning. Some research indicates that people hold their breath while learning, sometimes up to 40 seconds at a time. You wouldn't want to tell empaths to stop learning, would you?*

A. Of course not. Notice the combination of factors involved in this Automatic Subconscious Alert.

- You are paying attention to the object of your unintentional, semi-conscious, Prolonged Unskilled Empath Merge.
- You are staring.
- You are holding your breath.

Having all three factors present at the same time? I think you'll agree that is different from learning.

Q. *So long as we're being technical, is there anything else you can explain about this Automatic Subconscious Alert?*

A. It is unique among all the other techniques and workarounds in the system of Empath Empowerment®. Automatic Subconscious Alert could be considered a form of post-hypnotic suggestion.

Developing this technique, I drew on my background as a hypnotism instructor, certified by the National Guild of Hypnotists.

Here's another technical point, one that can make sense right away, without your having to become a professional hypnotist. If you reread the language created to install your Automatic Subconscious Alert, it explained that you would receive an alert only if you were doing unskilled empath merge.

That's important. For instance, not included are other random times of holding your breath, such as "Email apnea."

Q. *Whoa! What is email apnea?*

A. Imagine this. (And maybe you won't have to try very hard to imagine.) You open up email for the first time in a while. Loads of emails are cluttering up your in-box. So you begin sorting through them, pressured for time, very focused, utterly absorbed.

Might you start holding your breath? That's common, whether we consciously notice this happening or not.

Unfortunately scientific research has demonstrated that breath holding like this — EMAIL APNEA —contributes significantly to stress-related diseases.

Apart from times of learning, unintentionally holding breath is not necessarily beneficial.

So, if you wish, you could go back over to "Install an Automatic Subconscious Alert" and do it one more time. Substitute "Email Apnea" for "unskilled empath merge."

CHAPTER 29

Breathing to Raise Your Vibrations

Brave Empath, I'm so excited to introduce you to our next technique in this Program for Empath Empowerment. I love this technique so much, it's like one of my best friends.

For now, Vibe-Raising Breaths will help you to turn your empath gifts OFF. Later these special breaths will prove indispensable for turning empath gifts ON (in *The Master Empath*).

Just do not use Vibe-Raising Breaths when your nose is stopped up from a cold, nor while breathing hard after a brisk jog.

What else do you need to know now? As usual for any of our techniques, sit comfortably. Keep writing equipment nearby. I recommend simple, old-fashioned pen and paper, unless you prefer to make a digital recording of your voice, text yourself, etc.

Technique: INTRO TO VIBE-RAISING BREATHS

When I teach you this technique right now, Brave Empath, it will be sandwiched between a simple kind of before-and-after picture. Other times, you can use Vibe-Raising Breaths differently.

Okay, here you go.

1. Sit comfortably. Close your eyes. Let this latest technique begin!
2. Gently pay attention to yourself. Be especially interested in your emotions right now. Name one or more. These have names like *happy, sad, scared, angry.*

3. Open your eyes. Write down this "Before Picture about Your Emotions." Close your eyes again.
4. Gently pay attention to your physical body. Notice how your right leg feels. Sure, this has names like *strong, sore, relaxed, fidgety, heavy.*
5. Open your eyes. Write down this "Before Picture about Your Physical Self." Close your eyes again.
6. Take one Vibe-Raising Breath. Breathe in through your nose, then out through your mouth, nice and slow and deep.
7. Take a second Vibe-Raising Breath. And then return to normal breathing.
8. Repeat steps 2-5, only this time you are writing down an "After Picture."
9. Think "Technique over." Open your eyes.

Look over what you wrote for your "Before-and-After Picture." Did anything change? That would count as an immediate result, wouldn't it?

Q&A. Intro to Vibe-Raising Breaths

Q. *How slow and deep is a Vibe-Raising Breath supposed to be? Should I count to a number like 10 seconds while doing it?*

A. Slowish. Deepish. Please don't count seconds or otherwise attempt to be precise. Simply direct the flow of air, taking one breath at a time: In through your nose, out through your mouth.

Q. *Why take only two of these breaths in a row? Why not do it all day long?*

A. Right, as if you really need another job to do all day long! Isn't your life complicated enough without adding fancy breathing tricks? Besides, Vibe-Raising Breaths are powerful. Two or three in a sequence is plenty.

Q. *Comparing my Before-and-After Picture, I found myself calmer, both emotionally and physically. Is this normal?*

A. Forget about normal. Please, tell me that you don't consider that the purpose of your life is persuading other people to call you "Normal."

Q. *OK, was I successful? Does the relaxation I felt afterwards mean that I achieved success with my Vibe-Raising Breaths?*

A. Relaxation is one way to tell you were successful. Sure, you can officially count this as a result. Well done!

Q. *My result was kind of the opposite. Comparing my Before-and-After Picture, I felt clearer, more alert. Even physically! Was that wrong?*

A. "Vibe-Raising Breaths" will gently alter consciousness to provide more of what you need for the flow of awareness.

Using common sense, how could it be "wrong" to feel clearer and more alert, even better physically? Although I do appreciate your asking!

Q. *What I noticed was different from either of my classmates here. After the breathing, I felt more confident. It was subtle, but I'm pretty sure that's true. Could an outcome of Vibe-Raising Breaths be more confidence?*

A. Certainly!

Q. *Now I'm really confused. Rose, please explain how one little technique could produce such a range of results? How could all these different outcomes be genuine results?*

A. Breathing techniques shift consciousness. Energetically, what happens in a Vibe-Raising Breath?

Eyes closed, while you are in technique, what happens is a bit different from usual.

When you take that long, slow, deep inhalation, your Crown Chakra receives a bit more prana, life force energy, chi, etc. This can result in more clarity of experience.

To be really technical, every time you take a Vibe-Raising Breath, you are opening up your Crown Chakra a little, compared to how it was before. Hence the name, Vibe-Raising Breath. You are raising your spiritual vibrations, just a bit. For keeps.

Q. How about the exhale?

A. Remember the context first. W.while taking that out-through-mouth breath, you are in technique, eyes closed.

Your exhale becomes part of a technique. So results are different from other versions of exhaling through your mouth, like panting because you just had a really fabulous kiss or whatever.

In a Vibe-Raising Breath, the exhale allows some STUFF to be released from your aura and subconscious mind. Not your deepest frozen blocks of STUFF from other lifetimes, but small frozen blocks of energy that were cluttering up your energy field.

Consequently, after a Vibe-Raising Breath you might feel a bit of relief, whether physically or emotionally. You get what you need.

And really, what could be better than that? Automatically getting just what you need, yes!

Maybe how you can appreciate why I think of Vibe-Raising Breaths as being like a really good friend.

CHAPTER 30

More Physical Self-Awareness, Yum!

Brave Empath, have you fallen in love with yourself even more, thanks to Vibe-Raising Breaths? Let's continue the trend.

Our next technique is called "Grounding Breaths." This is another simple yet powerful breathing technique with many uses in this Program for Empath Empowerment.

Before doing the technique officially, with Q&A to follow, let's practice physical positioning.

Prepare Physically For Grounding Breaths

As you can appreciate, Brave Empath, there is a difference between doing a technique that shifts consciousness versus practicing a physical position.

This is our first time practicing such a position. Couldn't happen to a nicer person — or with a nicer technique!

- Hold up one index finger several inches in front of your mouth. Pretend it is a candle on your birthday cake. Yes, this is one of those (Funny? Obnoxious?) trick candles that won't blow out normally.
- Your practice, your job will be to huff and puff to blow out that imaginary candle flame, using one quick little breath at a time: Puff. Pause. Puff.
- For this position practice, I would like you to keep your eyes open, staring at that candle (or finger). For a few seconds, breathe in and out through your mouth.

- Now alter the rhythm, making your inhales and exhales short and forceful; puffy little breaths as if trying to blow that candle out. Take 5-10 of those quick little breaths, emphasizing the exhale, mouth open for the whole time.

Got it? Then you are prepared to do the technique for "Grounding Breaths." What will be different when doing the technique below? Your eyes will be closed. No uplifted finger. No associations required with obnoxious candles, either.

When not just practiced as a position — but done within a technique — "Grounding Breaths" move consciousness powerfully.

In the instructions that follow, you will take just two of those fun little breaths, pausing for a second between them. Afterwards return to normal breathing.

What will this technique do for you Let's find out.

Technique: INTRODUCTION TO GROUNDING BREATHS

1. Sit comfortably. Close your eyes. Let this latest technique begin!
2. Gently pay attention to yourself. Be especially interested in your emotions right now. Name one or more. Emotions have names like *happy, sad, scared, angry.*
3. Open your eyes. Write down this "Before Picture about Your Emotions." Close your eyes again.
4. Gently pay attention to your physical body. Notice how your left hand feels. Sure, this has names like *strong, sore, relaxed, fidgety, heavy.*
5. Open your eyes. Write down this "Before Picture about Your Physical Self." Close your eyes again.
6. Take two Grounding Breaths, pausing a second between each one. Breathe in and out through your mouth, rapidly, as if blowing out a candle. Emphasis will be on the exhale.

Take just two of these special, fancy breaths; then return to normal breathing.

7. Repeat steps 2-5, only this time you are writing down an "After Picture."
8. Think "Technique over." Open your eyes.

Look over what you wrote for your "Before-and-After Picture." Did anything change? That would count as an immediate result.

Q&A. Introduction to Grounding Breaths

Q. *This didn't feel like some deep technique to move consciousness. It felt pretty surfacey, frankly. Why would this count as a technique?*

A. Different techniques suit different purposes. Your question contains an important insight. "Grounding Breaths" help a person to "Shallow up." That is exactly the point.

Empath merges are deep, whether unskilled or skilled. As you progress in this Program for Empath Empowerment, you will learn a great deal about the value of shallow, surface, objective reality.

Q. *Physically, this breathing pattern made me feel more in my body. I don't know how else to describe it. Subtle. But a shift was definitely noticeable to me.*

What if I don't like how that feels, being more present within my body?

A. Get used to it. Many a talented empath floats around in consciousness, exploring other people, more interested in others than oneself. That habit stinks.

At least it can be changed. Glad you are taking advantage of this Program for Empath Empowerment!

Fact is, unskilled empaths can have a pretty, tenuous connection to the physical body. Or to objective reality in general. (Sadly, this habit does not necessarily include knowing there is a problem.)

Seems to me, you're just starting to change this, which definitely can feel a bit uncomfortable during the transition phase.

Keep going anyway. Pretty soon you can feel way more comfortable, effortlessly becoming more present to physical reality.

Q. *But why bother? Ignorance is bliss, right?*

A. Practical benefits, like more effectiveness in life — that's why it's worthwhile to progress through a bit of transitional awkwardness.

Another reason to land in your physical body more securely? As with the rest of Empath Empowerment, you will learn to feel like yourself, only clearer and stronger.

"Grounding Breaths" aren't just a theory. No more than having your consciousness grounded in the physical body is simply "a point of view." Having consciousness anchored in the physical body is very helpful indeed.

Want even more motivation to pursue body awareness as a way of life? Becoming more embodied can help you to gain credibility with family members and people at work. Could help you make more money. Might even improve your sex life.

Many clients and students of mine have reported such changes. If this were possible, wouldn't you like it to happen to you?

Q. *But what if I don't like paying attention to my physical body? What if it seems gross to me?*

A. You might benefit from doing "Introduction to Grounding Breaths" once or twice a day until you start feeling more comfortable in your body.

Body awareness does not have horrible side effects, like taking away your sensitivity. This positioning of consciousness is good for you as an empath. Beyond that, becoming more present, physically, can accelerate your personal development in many other ways.

Q. *Isn't it possible that I will never really feel comfortable with "Grounding Breaths"?*

A. "Never" is too long to wait for good results. After a couple of weeks, if you're still pretty uncomfortable in your own skin, seek out the services of a healing professional in energy spirituality or energy psychology. If extremely uncomfortable, invest in an evaluation by a psychiatrist.

Q. *I love how this technique made me feel, more solid and sure of myself. Is there a way I could safely use "Grounding Breaths" to help me turn empath gifts OFF?*

A. So glad you asked!

CHAPTER 31

A Human Reality App

Brave Empath, you have been developing the skills needed for "Coming Home," our big, fancy technique to turn your empath gifts OFF. One of those skills is "Grounding Breaths." You just learned basics for that in our last chapter.

Now I'll teach you a new use for this breathing pattern. Consider it an app, if you like. So handy if your lifestyle includes any kind of spiritual exercise! For example:

- You might take time for meditation, prayer, reading uplifting materials like scripture or your favorite blog.
- Self-hypnosis is popular, too, deservedly so. Many self-actualizing people regularly do that, or use techniques for creative visualization, listening to relaxing CDs, and so forth.
- Maybe you spend minutes at a time speaking out affirmations or asking "What Would Jesus Do?" or seeking wisdom from some other source that inspires you.
- You might participate in energy-based exercise, like yoga or tai chi.

What do practices like these have in common?

They position your consciousness away from regular human-level objective reality. Afterwards, it is common for empaths to become floaty. And floaty means — you guessed it — doing more unskilled empath merges than ever.

The following technique will protect you by smoothing the transition as you emerge from a spiritual practice.

Technique. A HUMAN-REALITY APP FOR GROUNDING BREATHS

Do the following immediately after finishing your meditation, yoga asanas, or any other kind of spiritual exercise.

Take a moment to recognize that your spiritual technique is over for now. You're returning to life as a human being, with regular human interests. Then:

1. Sit comfortably. Close your eyes. Let this different kind of technique begin!
2. Gently pay attention to yourself, in an easy and casual way. Be especially interested in your emotions right now. Name one or more. Emotions have names like *happy, sad, scared, angry.*
3. Open your eyes. Write down this "Before Picture about Your Emotions." Close your eyes again.
4. Gently pay attention to your physical body. Notice how your left hand feels. Sure, this has names like *strong, sore, relaxed, fidgety, heavy.*
5. Open your eyes. Write down this "Before Picture about Your Physical Self." Close your eyes again.
6. Take two Grounding Breaths, pausing a second between each one. Breathe in and out through your mouth, rapidly, as if blowing out a candle. Emphasis will be on the exhale. Take just two of these special breaths; then return to normal breathing.
7. Repeat steps 2-35 only this time you are writing down an "After Picture."
8. Think "Technique over."

Open your eyes. Review what you wrote for your "Before-and-After Picture." Did anything change? That would count as an immediate result.

Reinsert yourself into objective reality. Move around. Touch physical objects. Talk or sing or hum or yodel. Welcome back to human reality!

Q&A. A Human-Reality App for Grounding Breaths

Q. *But Rose, this technique is almost exactly identical to the last one, "Introduction to Grounding Breaths." What's the point?*

A. Context is the point, transitioning out of a spiritual practice. This can be a vulnerable time for us empaths because consciousness was positioned so differently during that spiritual exercise.

We empaths don't need much encouragement to continue traveling around, with random unskilled empath merges to follow.

Q. *What does this little bit of breathing have to do with consciousness? It's really just breathing, if you're honest.*

A. For 10,000 years or longer, wisdom traditions have linked breathing techniques to shifts in consciousness and changing a person's aura.

With today's energetic literacy, we can easily research what breathing techniques really accomplish. I'm one of the people who has done just that.

Returning from a really sweet prayer or other spiritual exercise, an afterglow is lovely. But spending the next few hours doing loads of unskilled empath merges? Not so lovely.

Avoid it with this "Human-Reality App for Grounding Breaths." You are more likely to stay put at human frequencies of experience, empath gifts nicely turned OFF. At least, for a while.

Q. *I'm sorta convinced. But I'd like to do a shortcut. I could just add those two puffy breaths at the end of my usual practice. Won't that be okay?*

A. It may be okay, in the sense that a couple of random puffy breaths will not harm you. After all, you have probably survived blowing out trick candles on a birthday cake long before this Program for Empath Empowerment.

However, if you do not do the full "Human-Reality App for Grounding Breaths," you are wasting your time for the purpose intended.

Thank you for introducing the important topic of putting energy-based techniques into perspective so that you can get the desired results.

CHAPTER 32

Self-Authority Versus Skills

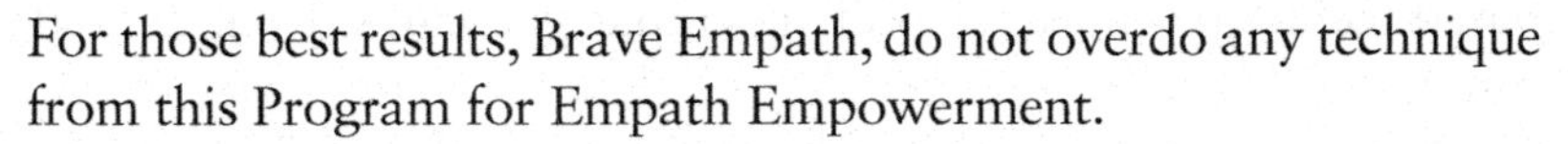

For those best results, Brave Empath, do not overdo any technique from this Program for Empath Empowerment.

This caution extends to overdoing techniques just because you like how they feel. Overdoing for any reason, actually. Overdoing means overdoing.

For example, let's compare "Introduction to Grounding Breaths" to adding some salt to your food. Sprinkling on a little, by doing the technique once or twice in your *day*? Fine. Doing that same technique many times every *hour*? That's like eating enough salt to pickle yourself.

Over-using any technique in this Program for Empath Empowerment is like ingesting too much salt or any other healthy substance... where some is great... but too much adds up to a problem.

As for under-using, that can lead to problems too. With any technique that I teach you, please, either do the entire technique or don't bother.

Ever since publication of *Empowered by Empathy* readers have come to me sheepishly, describing how they wrecked techniques for themselves.

Wrecked unintentionally, of course. Of course, my students didn't literally put it that way. Jessica might complain, "Your technique doesn't work anymore."

On inquiry, it turned out that she had made up their own version of mix-and-match, like walking down the street while checking text messages and taking the occasional Vibe-Raising Breath.

Please, never!

Never take one piece of a technique and use that separately, tossing away the rest of the technique sequence. No part of a technique is optional, not in the Program for Empath Empowerment, anyway.

Random experiments don't just disrespect your teacher and the enormous amount of research that goes into every technique I present to you. No, you would be disrespecting yourself. While simultaneously wrecking a technique's further effectiveness for you.

Doesn't Self-Authority Rule?

Self-authority can be tricky. It matters enormously for Empath Empowerment, as for every aspect of personal life. Yet self-authority doesn't equate to knowledge, expertise, or skill.

Creativity feels good. Yet good feelings alone don't automatically make us experts. Did the creativity feel good just because it felt good to your self-authority, as in "I did it myself?" Or was skill involved, too?

In this Program for Empath Empowerment, you are learning loads of practical, relevant skills. Not included, though? How to become a CONSCIOUSNESS ENGINEER, a spiritual teacher who specializes in designing effective techniques.

So, if you're wise:

- Use self-authority to evaluate skill sets being taught. Do you wish to learn that skill, taught in that particular way, from that particular teacher?
- Once the skill set is learned, use your self-authority to decide when and how to use it.
- Also, after giving any skill set a fair chance, use self-authority to evaluate what really works for you.

All this is different from tinkering with the basic skills themselves.

Traveling into an Analogy

Here's an analogy to clarify the difference. Learning to drive a car is a skill. Once you develop that skill, you can use self-authority to decide when and where to drive a car.

By contrast, there are separate engineering skill sets for learning how to design an automobile. Unless you learn these skills, here's a goofy example of what could happen.

Oliver has great skills as a driver, plus loads of self-authority. He can use this combination to choose the route he drives to work, find great parking spaces, even improvise a road trip.

But what if Oliver starts thinking like this? "Hey, I know how to drive. I deal with this car every day, and it moves slower than it used to. I ought to be able to fix that. Sure, I feel confident I can fix this problem. I own the car, don't I?"

So here's his solution, fueled by self-authority. Oliver opens up the hood of his car to add a few missing ingredients. "I know how it feels to go fast. I've just got to figure out what would help my car feel the same way. How about one of my old skateboards? That ought to help. What, it's too big? I'll break it into a couple of pieces."

After tossing that in, Oliver thinks, "Wait, going faster like that might be tricky for my engine. What else can I do? Of course! I'll add a padlock, to keep everything safe."

Oliver feels so good about his improvements to the car, he wonders what more he might add. "Maybe that slow performance is an attitude problem. How can I get my car to know that my time is valuable? I guess the best way to do that is to throw in a sports watch."

Ooooookay.

Finally, just to be on the safe side, Oliver hurls in a wire whisk from the kitchen.

"My wife used to use that for cooking, but I can always get her another one. Now this old tool has a new job, teaching all the other car parts how to mix it up. In you go, whisk. Help the old parts of my car to get along with all of these other improvements."

Then Oliver closes the hood, proud of his first foray into car mechanics. At his current skill level, everything he has done makes perfect sense to him. Self-authority galore.

Ridiculous example? Sure. Unfortunately, inexpertly designed techniques are common in real life. Results are not funny, either. I know because sometimes my job is to help clients to clean up the resulting mess.

Problems from poorly designed self-improvement techniques don't show obviously, like fictional Oliver playing around with his car right before it explodes. Instead, problems develop at their own pace in the subconscious mind, maybe not obvious to Oliver for 10 years, 30 years, or later. Finally he goes "OUCH!"

Delayed timing doesn't make such problems trivial.

Here's the practical point for now; about reality rather than fiction.

Ultimately it is your responsibility what you do with this Program for Empath Empowerment. So be smart with your choices, Brave Empath. And don't confuse self-authority with skills.

Get real skills, then evaluate the results with your self-authority. That's the perfect combo.

For Empath Empowerment, you have accomplished a great deal with our breathing techniques. Now let's carry this productive momentum forward.

CHAPTER 33

Explore Your Human Life, Divinely Protected

Our next technique will subtly expand your consciousness. Brave Empath, I will teach you a way to connect your consciousness to a transpersonal source of huge joy, wisdom, and love.

To prepare, find the usual tiny chunk of time when you will be uninterrupted. Also choose one name for the Divine to use for this particular exploration of the technique.

- You might choose the **Impersonal Aspect** of the Divine, such as God, Allah, Holy Spirit, The Love That Rules the Universe, or The Intelligence That Rules the Universe.
- Or you might choose a **Personal Aspect** of the Divine, either an Ascended Master or an Archangel.
- **Ascended Masters** include Jesus, Krishna, Buddha, Kwan Yin, Athena, Isis.
- **Archangels** include Archangel Michael, Archangel Gabriel, Archangel Raphael.

Every time you use the following technique, pick one Divine Being to help you.

Once you have made your choice, prepare for doing a technique as usual, including your quick read-through in advance.

Technique. GET BIG

Welcome to one of my all-time favorite techniques, Brave Empath.

1. Sit comfortably. Close your eyes. Let this latest technique begin!
2. Gently pay attention to yourself, in an easy and casual way. Be especially interested in your emotions right now. Name one or more. Sure, these have names like *happy, sad, scared, angry.*
3. Open your eyes. Write down this "Before Picture about Your Emotions." Close your eyes again.
4. Gently pay attention to your physical body. Notice how your upper back feels. Sure, this has names *like strong, sore, relaxed, fidgety, heavy.*
5. Open your eyes. Write down this "Before Picture about Your Physical Self." Close your eyes again.
6. Think, just once, the name you will use this time, doing Get Big. For example, you might think "The Love That Rules the Universe."
7. Immediately after, take two Vibe-Raising Breaths. Then return to normal breathing.
8. Repeat steps 2-5, only this time you are writing down an "After Picture."
9. Think "Technique over."

Open your eyes. Look over what you wrote for your "Before-and-After Picture." Did anything change? That would count as an immediate result.

Q&A. Get Big

Q. *Does it always have to be the same choice of Divine Being?*

A. No. You're doing a technique, not getting a tattoo.

Q. *What happens after you open your eyes at the end? Do you stay energetically Big?*

A. Gradually your conscious mind will shrink back to its usual identity, much like a rubber band that has been stretched beyond its ordinary limits. This could take hours or minutes. For sure, the shift will be gentle and appropriate for your current level of consciousness.

Q. *Wouldn't it be great to do this all day long?*

A. Hardly! Overdoing is not recommended with this technique or any other part of this Program for Empath Empowerment. For jobs like driving to work, walking the dog, or cleaning the bathroom, we do fine with our everyday little minds.

I wouldn't recommend using "Get Big" as a way of life. It could space you out, the opposite of being an effective, skilled empath. Instead use this technique as recommended in our Program for Empath Empowerment.

Q. *Why use a name for the Divine. Isn't It smart enough to know what I mean without asking? Why can't I just ask the Universe?*

A. You can. Only you will not be doing the "Get Big" technique and cannot expect the same kind of protection for your explorations as an empath.

Q. *How about calling on your guardian angel or spirit guides?*

A. Same answer.

Q. *What if calling on anyone goes against your religion?*

A. Then don't think of this technique as religious. Think of it as convenience. You might want to reread this short chapter. Will you find anything here about bowing down, worshipping in any other way, believing in anything?

Personally I find that "Get Big" is a pretty good deal, whether you believe in a religion or not. You ask for help in a particular way, no strings attached. Then you receive that help. Not too many people would do that for you but God will.

Q. *I was unprepared for what a powerful experience it was for me, doing "Get Big." What are some ways I can use this to become more skilled as an empath?*

A. Glad you asked....

Recommended Uses for "Get Big"

This little technique has innumerable uses because it is a super-easy way to co-create with the Divine. You will find loads of uses as part of other trademarked systems I teach and write about For sure, the system of Empath Empowerment depends upon using the awesome resource of your Divine connection.

Besides being so effortless, "Get Big" is flexible because belief is not needed, nor faith, nor belonging to any particular religious community.

You can even think of this resource as your own Higher Self. Just don't employ that name for Divine Being when doing "Get Big." As with 12-step programs, it is essential to have help outside yourself. (Incidentally, unlike 12-step programs, it won't be enough to use the term "Higher Power." Make that "Highest Power." You deserve that much.)

In the Program for Empath Empowerment, this tiny technique is a component of more complex techniques that turn empath gifts OFF. (Coming soon.)

CHAPTER 34

Wake Up Your Sense of Self

Brave Empath, being an unskilled empath can feel like a Catch 22. While unskilled, you are constantly picking up STUFF from others. So long as your aura is riddled with STUFF, it's hard to feel like yourself.

Until you strengthen that sense of self, what happens? Automatically, you keep picking up STUFF, like a random drip-drip-drip.

Such a vicious cycle, being an unskilled empath! But hold on. That cycle has stopped spinning around quite so fast.

- By now, you understand that you really have gifts, not some nightmarish disability. Clarity has grown. Your *sense of self* can be understood as something different from *problems* formerly suffered due to lack of skill.
- You were given a model for understanding what has been happening to you energetically. Therefore you can stop "Blaming the victim." You're beginning to appreciate that you can also stop *being* a victim.
- You have learned techniques to break old habits of doing Prolonged Unskilled Empath Merges.
- In our last chapter, I taught you a no-frills way to co-create with the Divine. That will become very helpful for breaking the vicious cycle where unskilled empath merges cause you to take on STUFF, resulting in random distortions to your sense of self, which then predisposes you to do even more unskilled empath merges.

Next comes a powerful technique that wakes up your sense of self by removing an empath's random STUFF. You will learn how to move out Imported STUFF from your aura right now, those globs and blobs of stuck energy that originally belonged to other people.

As you may squirmingly remember, taking on random STUFF is the inevitable consequence of doing unskilled empath merge.

No need to blame yourself; the whole process happened subconsciously. Consciously, you are learning how to stop that cycle, one technique at a time.

Technique: EMPATH'S FIRST AID

Our latest technique will include "Get Big." So decide which name you will choose this time around. Will your choice be an Ascended Master or Archangel? Perhaps you will prefer to use a name for the impersonal aspect of the Divine.

In the steps that follow, I will use the name "God." Substitute your choice every time.

- Sit comfortably and close your eyes.
- Notice what it is like to be you, right now. No judging, please. Just pay attention as someone who is interested in you. Choose something about your current emotions or physical sensations in your body or anything at all that you notice about yourself.
- Open your eyes just long enough to write something down. Then close your eyes.
- Open your eyes long enough to read the following sequence of words, saying them out loud:

God, remove from my aura whatever does not belong to me.

Remove from my aura whatever does not belong to me.

Remove from my aura whatever does not belong to me.

Fill me with new love, light, and power.

- Repeat Steps 2 and 3.
- End the technique. Think something like "Technique over" or "Thanks, God." Open your eyes.

Look at what you wrote down. Comparing your Before-and-After, do you notice anything different?

When to Use Empath's First Aid

Now that you have learned the technique, when is a good time to do it? For the next week or so, use the technique as often as twice daily, maybe once around lunchtime and once after dinner.

Just that couple of times will get you accustomed to the contrast. Because unskilled empath merges do tend to sneak up on a person.

Count this as education. It's important to get a sense of being yourself, separate from taking on STUFF from others.

After a couple of weeks, use this technique only when you feel the need. That might amount to a couple of times a week.

Q&A. Empath's First Aid

Q. *Strangely I do feel better, almost a sense of relief. But why?*

A. Subconscious experiences can be almost noticeable consciously, like the saying, "What I want to say is on the tip of my tongue."

Even though hidden in the subconscious mind, Imported STUFF can bother you enough to be vaguely noticed consciously. And now, consciously, you noticed the contrast.

Q. *But I didn't feel better. I felt grumpy before I started. Now I'm just as grumpy. Does that mean the "Empath's First Aid" didn't work?*

A. No, it just means that this particular technique was not sufficient to heal other kinds of subconscious STUFF that are bothering you now. "Empath's First Aid" will also fail to fix your broken computer, restore your dog Fido to perfect health, and remove all other causes of grumpiness.

Q. *I didn't notice any result, either. Honestly, wasn't I wasting my time?*

A. A technique like this is a resource to bring you results over time. Every moment of education need not be thrilling. Give this technique a chance. Use it for a week. Twice daily. Then evaluate, okay?

Q. *Look, I want my Empath Empowerment to be simple. I would like to stop right here. Why not only use "Empath's First Aid"? Couldn't that be all I need to turn my empath gifts OFF? Why not just use this STUFF-removal technique once an hour?*

A. An ounce of prevention is worth a pound of cure. "Empath's First Aid" is for cure. Soon you will learn "Coming Home," which is for prevention. Fix now, prevent soon. That's our strategy.

Q. *When I'm in a hurry, I can just use the words in "Empath's First Aid," right? Admit it. The rest of the sequence you just gave us — isn't that just padding?*

A. I respect all you empaths far too much to include padding. This is not done with any technique I design.

You know, in plenty of life situations, it's a matter of personal taste how thorough you are about doing things. Perhaps you never wish to have any conversation longer than a tweet. Someone else might feel terribly deprived that way, believing that genuine intimacy takes longer than a tweet. Up to you, though! With such choices, self-authority rules.

Remember the earlier discussion of self-authority not replacing skills, like Oliver as a car mechanic? "Empath's First Aid" will lose its full effectiveness for you by being changed, used out of context, or just sampled.

Consider yourself warned. Don't cut-and-paste portions of "Empath's First Aid." Do the full technique. Then you will enjoy the full results.

CHAPTER 35

Appreciate Your Multi-Level Humanity

Brave Empath, you can handle the ideas in this chapter. You can handle these ideas because you are both an empath and courageous.

Not that I'm calling other people cowards, necessarily. More like squeamish.

Human life is messy, humbling, complicated — whether we consciously admit that or not. Becoming skilled as an empath, you are going to learn much more about your human life than you have known so far, discovering many new insights about yourself.

This chapter will complete our preparation for "Coming Home," the most important technique for turning empath gifts OFF in this Program for Empath Empowerment. If you can handle reading this entire chapter without throwing up, I'd say the odds are excellent that you can become a fully skilled empath.

Teasing! Every empath can become fully skilled. It just takes a willingness to show some adventurousness, take a bit of time, learn some skills.

Fortunately, there is no instant way to stop all pain as an empath and, instead, awaken the full potential of your empath gifts.

What's so fortunate about that? A deep learning about yourself is required to satisfactorily turn OFF empath gifts. Automatically this can also help you progress extra-fast on your path of personal development. Besides, getting to know yourself better can be fun.

Celebrate Your Amazing Individuality

Unique in all the universe, and different from any incarnation you have had in the long history of your soul, wow! There really is nobody like you, nor will there ever be.

Part of the fun is that, since you're human, your individuality contains many levels. Well, Brave Empath, I'm going to teach you a step-by-step way to explore all five of the most significant levels of your individuality. What are these five different levels within? For clarity, let's start with...

Three Things You Are NOT

None of the following is a legitimate level to consider when probing for an empath's experience of who-you-be.

1. You are not your history

Instead, you *have* a history. Common sense suggests it would be limiting to define your present self (and future potential) in terms of what you have been through so far. Yet isn't it tempting to label yourself, based on experiences from your past? For example:

- I'm successful in my career.
- I'm not successful in my career.
- I have a fulfilling love relationship.
- I can't seem to get my love life together.
- I own a fine, shiny automobile.
- My car is a pathetic old clunker.
- I am the product of a dysfunctional family.
- I am a recovering alcoholic.
- I have financial troubles.
- My spiritual teacher told me that I am saved/awake/chosen/psychically gifted.
- I am a great parent.

Could such versions of reality be true? Would it be smart to believe any of them is your big defining characteristic? Could believing strongly in this distort your sense of who you are right now? Sure, sure not, sure.

All of these bits of history are *ideas*, not *experiences* of how your consciousness functions in the here and now. None will be relevant for the "Coming Home" technique.

Beliefs like these will neither help nor hinder your becoming a skilled empath.

2. You are not other people's reactions to you

Not unless you truly desire to drive yourself nuts.

One thing I will say for basing self-concept on how other people treat you: It can be a very interesting experiment for all or part of an incarnation. Could be a game you have played for many past incarnations, actually.

What's the payoff? For one thing, drama galore.

However, skill as an empath requires no drama. And for you to position consciousness appropriately as an empath, it isn't relevant how other people treat you.

Until you develop an appropriate, nuanced appreciation for yourself as a person, other people's opinions of you will matter way too much for comfort.

Fortunately, nobody else is authorized to turn your sense of self ON, or to turn your empath gifts appropriately OFF during most of your waking hours.

You are hired, though. (If you want to be.)

3. You are not your lifestyle

Sure, your lifestyle *matters*. But changes to lifestyle help empaths only after becoming quite skilled. Lifestyle changes alone will never create a skilled empath.

If you have done certain techniques for self-improvement, or been in therapy, you may have the habit of observing yourself rather than spontaneously being yourself, saying and doing whatever suits the occasion.

Has self-consciousness become a habit? Then let it go for a few weeks. I invite you to such an experiment, a quiet call to innocence.

Neither self-conscious monitoring of behavior nor consciously adjusting personal boundaries will do the job of the "Coming Home" technique. This will give you an opportunity to taste this hidden aspect of life. You will spend a short time at each level of self, gently paying attention. Then you can experience directly how your consciousness flows at each vibrational level of your human personality.

Acceptance can result. Acceptance means experiencing yourself just the way you are right now: No forcing yourself to change or improve in any way.

What, notice yourself directly, without fixing a thing? This can wake you up as a soul, awaken you even more powerfully than the not-too-shabby technique you recently learned for "Empath's First Aid."

You Are Not Just One or Two Preferred Levels of Yourself, Either

Although here is where many empaths get tripped up. Even if you are already savvy about consciousness, philosophical self-knowledge, psychological inquiry, financial planning, human history, animal husbandry, deep sea diving, whatever.

You are *every one* of the levels of you that will be discussed in the rest of this chapter. Not just one, and definitely not only what you prefer. Every single level built into your human system really does count. Even if understandably you will always have some favorites.

By way of analogy, which do you like better, Brave Empath, your head or your left elbow?

So glad you don't have to choose! Both count as part of you, and you do get to keep them both. Meaning no disrespect to your noble head, it really is fine to continue owning your elbow.

To understand your depth identity as a human, let's shift from this analogy to consider....

Five Different Levels of Your Sweet Self

Yes, let's take inventory of who you are now. In this chapter, we'll get the concepts together. Next chapter, when you actually *do* the "Coming Home" technique, you will be invited to experience of each level in succession.

Every experience will involve a moment of gently paying attention. Afterwards, you will be invited to write down something quickly, as with the Before-and-After notes you took while doing techniques for "Intro to Vibe-Raising Breaths" and "Introduction to Grounding Breaths."

What exactly are these levels? Just because you *have* them subconsciously doesn't mean that you necessarily know about them consciously. So, yes, let's consider.

Level One: Social

You have a way of being yourself, here and now. Which is the case through all your waking hours, even if your social situation changes and, with it, your way of being you.

Where you are does not mean the same thing as *who* you are. Yet some environments do make you feel more comfortable than others, right? In some situations you feel more resourceful, more clever or popular or attractive. Even where you live, different rooms might arouse different feelings within you about self-worth and your importance to others.

Wherever you happen to be while doing "Coming Home," that will be your current environment in objective reality.

- Are you alone at home with this book?
- Perhaps you are visiting a difficult relative and have captured some precious time alone, locked in the guest room for the express purpose of exploring yourself on your own terms.
- Alternatively you could be sitting with one favorite friend, exploring this book together, eagerly preparing to do "Coming Home."
- Or you might be a graduate of this Program for Empath Empowerment, having gone through this book more than once. Now you're preparing to deepen your knowledge and experiences.

Wherever you are in objective reality, you have a related social self. So that is the first level you will explore.

However it feels to be you, in any way — while you're in technique that particular time — this is what you will be exploring at the level of your social self.

Level Two: Physical

Sometimes you might be more aware physically than at other times. Hey, for an entire *incarnation* you might be more aware physically, compared to other past lifetimes. Just the opposite could be true as well. However interested you are in your body right now, it does count as one of your levels of self.

Gently paying attention there, while in technique, your self-confidence and intelligence and comfort could be entirely different from what you have at Level One, The Social Level.

Usually we don't give a thought to which level of self is working well and which is not. We're too busy participating. But for the "Coming Home" technique, you will bring awareness to being yourself at each one of the five levels. No wonder these subtle experiences can become a quiet revelation.

Level Three: Mental

Thinking. That's the common denominator for your signature experience at this inner level. But what does it mean, having that abstract experience called "Thinking"? For you, Brave Empath, thinking could include:

- Words that you hear inwardly
- Images or cartoons that you see inwardly
- Abstract textures to your experience
- Strongly held opinions
- Thoughts about your thoughts
- How much you like learning, right now
- How comfortable and confident you feel about learning in general

The technique you'll learn here allows for all of this to count. At any given time, you will have some degree of comfort and confidence with your own thinking process. While exploring, your job will be to gently notice this... whatever. Not to judge, not to fix. Simply to notice.

Level Four: Emotional

Consciously, Brave Empath, you always have at least one underlying emotion. Happens automatically.

But consciously *noticing* that you have an emotion? Now that's another story. Not every empath has had much experience at purposely noticing and naming emotions.

Emotions do not have to include big drama, like the degree of intensity we expect from watching TV. Emotions can be recognized as words that you hear in your head or a feeling that crosses your mind.

In the "Coming Home" technique, noticing your emotions does not have to be mushy-gushy and loaded with feelings. It's just info.

Also, emotions do not have to make intellectual sense. Nor do they have to fit together logically. It is absolutely human to feel conflicting emotions simultaneously, like:

- Both joyful and impatient
- Both proud of yourself and ashamed of yourself
- Both calm, curious, and anxious
- Both worried, secure, furious, and superior to others

When doing "Coming Home," at The Emotional Level, you will write down the series of emotions, whatever it is. Or the one emotion, whatever it is.

Or you might write down something about the *flow of emotions*, like fascinated by my emotions, overwhelmed by all the feelings, emotionally numb.

Just write it down, not doing anything more complicated than that.

Level Five: Spiritual

Spiritual experience for you could be about silence. Or space. Or light. Or colors. Or shifting energy.

You might have an emotion, and that would count, too.

Perhaps you might sense a presence. Whatever! Please trust your self-authority enough to count whatever you experience. Count it enough to write it down.

Of course, just like any other level of self, you could have experiences at the spiritual level that don't necessarily seem relevant at all, such as:

- Physically tense
- Hard to think

- Feeling uncertain, not trusting myself
- Noticing a lot of energy
- Time seems to move really slowly, and not in a comfortable way

Positive or negative, exalted or mundane, please remember that everything counts when exploring a level of yourself. It is what it is, just for now.

Also, any experience you have at this time could be completely different tomorrow.

Whenever you do the "Coming Home" technique, your goal is not to find patterns or evaluate yourself. You will simply notice whatever you happen to notice, then write down a quick summary.

Techniques to move consciousness, or turn OFF empath gifts, are not designed to meet other needs as well. If you want to do religious studies, do them separately. If you seek entertainment, go to the movies.

Exploring yourself at the spiritual level can feel different from each of the other levels. Why wouldn't it? Each of these five levels is distinctive and important. That's right, Brave Empath. Each of your levels of self is both distinctive and important.

None of them matters more than the others, at least not for the sake of waking you up from the inside. Automatically this will turn your empath gifts OFF for hours to come.

CHAPTER 36

"Coming Home," Our Most Important Technique

If you hadn't been prepared so systematically, you might find it tricky to do the "Coming Home" technique.

Now? It can be simple and effortless. Brave Empath, you are thoroughly prepared to have a fresh experience every time that you use this technique.

Just to remind you, although each experience of "Coming Home" can be fascinating, having fun with it is not the point. Which is turning your empath gifts OFF, bringing about wonderful results in an empath's life.

Here's an overview of what we'll be doing. In the following sequence of technique steps I will guide you through brief exploration of five essential layers within. You will experience each one in turn.

- Moving inwardly through progressively deeper levels, you will be propelled by taking just one Vibe-Raising Breath at the appropriate time.
- Outward bound, you will take one Grounding Breath as directed.

Overall, your job will be simple. Notice things without trying to change them. Then write a few scribble notes.

So get your writing equipment handy, Brave Empath. On that page, or computer document, write the following sequence of words. Leave space in-between for the scribble notes.

1. Social
2. Physical
3. Mental
4. Emotional
5. Spiritual
6. Emotional
7. Mental
8. Physical
9. Social

Technique: COMING HOME

So, you have prepared your note-taking equipment by listing all nine categories. And did you take reasonable precautions against being interrupted? Superb, you Brave Empath!

Read through the following and then you're good to go. Take it one step at a time. (Open one eye and peek at these steps, as needed.) Allow 15-20 minutes the first few times you go through this "Coming Home" technique. With practice, you can do the sequence faster, as will be discussed later. For now, enjoy taking your time, getting to know you-know-who.

1. Sit comfortably and close your eyes. To help yourself wake up inwardly, Get Big. Then take one Vibe-Raising Breath. You are preparing to learn more about yourself.
2. Right now, Brave Empath, awareness is positioned at your social self. How does it feel to be you right now? What do you notice? Find some words and open your eyes long enough to write down a few scribble notes. Then close your eyes.
3. Although it is interesting to keep your consciousness positioned at this level, your consciousness is fluid and flexible. Effortlessly your awareness can shift to different positioning. In a moment, with eyes closed, take one Vibe-Raising Breath. Continue to sit with eyes closed, breathing normally. Automatically your awareness will travel to the next level inward, which is your physical self. The shift in consciousness will be effortless. Take that breath now.
4. Right now, Brave Empath, awareness is positioned at your physical self. How does it feel to be you right now? What

do you notice? Find some words and open your eyes long enough to write down a few scribble notes. Then close your eyes.

5. Although it is interesting to keep your consciousness positioned at this level, your consciousness is fluid and flexible. In a moment, with eyes closed, you will take one Vibe-Raising Breath. Continue to sit with eyes closed, breathing normally. Automatically your awareness will travel to the next level inward, which is your mental functioning, mind and intellect. Take that breath now.
6. So now, Brave Empath, awareness is positioned at your mental level. How does it feel to be you right now? What do you notice? Find some words and open your eyes long enough to write a few scribble notes. Then close your eyes.
7. Although it is interesting to keep your consciousness positioned at this level, your consciousness is fluid and flexible. You will find it effortless to travel in consciousness to the next level inward, which is your emotional self. In a moment, with eyes closed, take one Vibe-Raising Breath. Continue to sit with eyes closed, breathing normally. Automatically your awareness will be positioned at this level of yourself. Take that breath now.
8. How familiar, Brave Empath! Your awareness is positioned at your emotional self. How does it feel to be you right now? What do you notice? Find some words and open your eyes long enough to write a few scribble notes. Then close your eyes.
9. Although it is interesting to keep your consciousness positioned at this level, your consciousness is fluid and flexible. You can easily travel in consciousness to the next destination for awareness, the next level inward, which is your spiritual self — who you are right now energetically. In a moment, with eyes closed, take one Vibe-Raising Breath. Continue to sit with eyes closed, breathing normally. Automatically your awareness will be positioned at this level of yourself. Take that breath now.

10. Yet another way of being yourself, Brave Empath! Awareness is positioned at *your spiritual self.* How does it feel to be you right now? What do you notice? Find some words and open your eyes long enough to write a few scribble notes. Then close your eyes. If you wish, linger at this level for a while. Then continue.
11. Now you can begin to travel outward in consciousness, one level at a time. Your next level to re-visit will be the one about your emotional self. In a moment, with eyes closed, take one Grounding Breath. Continue to sit with eyes closed, breathing normally. Automatically your awareness will be positioned at this level. Take that breath now.
12. Here you are, with awareness positioned at *your emotional self.* How does it feel to be you right now? What do you notice? Find some words and open your eyes long enough to write a few scribble notes. Then close your eyes.
13. Next to experience, moving in consciousness, is your mental self: In a moment, with eyes closed, take one Grounding Breath. Continue to sit with eyes closed, breathing normally. Automatically your awareness will be positioned at this level of yourself. Take that breath now.
14. Here you are, with awareness positioned at *your mental self.* How does it feel to be you right now? What do you notice? Find some words and open your eyes long enough to write a few scribble notes. Then close your eyes.
15. Which level will come next? The level of your physical self. In a moment, with eyes closed, take one Grounding Breath. Continue to sit with eyes closed, breathing normally. Automatically your awareness will be positioned at the level of your physical body. Take that breath now.
16. Here you are, Brave Empath. Your entire body has come back. Go from feet to head. Check out how your full body is there. Just the sort of thing that you are well

positioned to notice with awareness at *your physical self.* How does it feel to be you right now? What do you notice? Find some words and open your eyes long enough to write a few scribble notes. Then close your eyes.

17. The final level for experience in the sequence you're doing right now is your social self, what you are like at the level of the environment. In a moment, with eyes closed, take 11 Grounding Breaths. Pace yourself comfortably. Avoid taking these breaths too fast. Afterwards continue to sit with eyes closed, breathing normally. Automatically your awareness will shift outward and you will start noticing yourself where you are sitting right now. Take all 11 breaths.
18. Now awareness is positioned at *your social self,* Brave Empath. Isn't it fascinating how you can start to notice furniture and other things about your environment? That can happen easily, even with eyes closed, while awareness is positioned at objective life, human reality. How does it feel to be you right now? What do you notice? Find some words and open your eyes long enough to write a few scribble notes. Then close your eyes.
19. Think "Technique over." Maybe also "Congratulations, I am definitely a Brave Empath." Open your eyes.

Look over your notes. What happened this time? No matter what you wrote down, so long as you followed all the steps of this technique, you did just fine.

Q&A. Coming Home

Q. *I love, love, love this technique. Except I didn't enjoy the body level. Or the mind level. Can I leave them out next time?*

A. Eventually you will love, love, love the experience of yourself at every one of these levels. At least that will be the overall pattern.

Each time you do "Coming Home," your experiences could be different. Each time, let your experience be what it is. To enjoy the benefits of the technique, experiencing each level is required. Here I won't go into more detail about results until our next chapter. Here let's continue to discuss doing the technique itself.

Q. *Was this supposed to be hard and give me a headache?*

A. No! When you're studying any technique in the Program for Empath Empowerment, take it easy. And keep breathing. Trying harder with how you use consciousness will never bring you extra success. If anything, you will create "benefits" like a headache, a stiff neck, or a general sense of frustration. Luckily, you don't need to push. "Coming Home" can be comfortable.

Q. *What if all the time you're supposed to be Coming Home you keep thinking about other people?*

A. Many empaths do that habitually. But remember, you're in the process of switching your empath talent OFF. No matter which way your stream of consciousness drifts, eventually a choice will become available. In that instant, *you will realize that you're thinking about other people rather than yourself.*

Only then do you have a choice. Right then, choose to pay attention to the level of self being explored during that step of the "Coming Home" technique. Returning to yourself, persistently but gently, will train you to put yourself first instead of putting others first.

Q. *That three-ring circus was The Real Me? Scary.*

A. Going within can be a shock, especially if you haven't had much practice. So much can be happening.

Nonstop motion is an illusion, though. With more experience, you'll find that familiarity brings content.

Meanwhile, here's my advice. Whenever you have a choice, go back to the level of self in that technique step that you're officially exploring. For instance, being interested in your physical body.

Q. *Could I be a Brave Empath but also a klutz at being self-aware?*

A. A Brave-But-Not-Completely-Skilled Empath? Sure. A Skilled Empath, no. Spontaneous awareness of yourself is required for becoming skilled.

Therefore, count yourself successful every time you do the technique for "Coming Home." Regardless of your experience this time, the process will help you to accept yourself more.

Q. *What if I noticed something really weird, like the fact that my head didn't seem connected to my body?*

A. Very important point about this technique: For best results don't try to fix a thing. Simply pay attention and then write down your scribble notes.

Q. *I thought maybe if I sent myself a little healing energy....*

A. Then you'd be doing a different technique. The power of *this* technique consists in your doing nothing except for a sloppy sort of paying attention, then writing down some words.

Paying attention to yourself, *as you are*, can be a powerful form of self-acceptance. Every empath, every person, needs plenty of that.

Q. *How does your technique for "Coming Home" differ from cutting yourself off from people?*

A. Context makes the difference. What you are doing here is a specific technique, done for a limited amount of time.

Q. *I think it would be more fun to play background music while doing this technique. Is that okay?*

A. No, definitely not okay. You might wish to record this technique. Read aloud one step at a time. Leave the same amount of time between each step. That time could range between 10-90 seconds, depending on how much depth of immersion you wish to experience. Just be consistent.

How will your life change if you do "Coming Home" every day for the next month? Experience can supply the best answer. Our next chapter will give you a preview... plus other information vital for keeping your empath gifts routinely, and effortlessly, turned OFF.

CHAPTER 37

Break out of the Amusement Park

THE AMUSEMENT PARK is my name for the lifestyle of an unskilled empath. A Disneyland for your consciousness, it's the opposite of staying home. Since you have 1 or more of the 15 empath gifts, you will find attractions galore at this fascinating playland.

Your amusement adventure happens in consciousness rather than physical reality. Neither do you pay for tickets nor must you wait in line. Regardless of how many other empaths might be in the crowd, your turn comes first every time. Instantly.

And the number of rides you can take is unlimited.

No wonder unskilled empaths routinely ride to the point of exhaustion.

Think about it: Free rides, all day, all night. So tempting to overdo! To make matters worse, pleasure is associated with these rides. Split-Split-Second Empath Merges, one after another, yum! Prolonged Unskilled Empath Merges, even more alluring. Unfortunately all this subconscious intrigue does not protect you from the inevitable, inadvertent Imported STUFF.

For instance, your best friend Brody's emotional wavelength is not obvious like a clattering roller coaster. So you may never have noticed that your consciousness goes riding on it whenever the two of you visit. Regardless, each amusement park ride on Brody's energies will bring you consequences that last long after that friendly time together.

Will bring you, not *may*. You *will* definitely receive some new Imported STUFF from Brody... every single time.

The following awareness regimen will help you to break out of the amusement park so you can return home at will. Live a more stable life, increasingly secure in your human identity.

By now, Brave Empath, you may appreciate more than ever why it is not responsible to learn Skilled Empath Merge until you have become very, very comfortable with keeping your empath gifts OFF.

With experience, you can adapt the "Coming Home" technique to work most quickly and conveniently. Here's how.

Adapt "Coming Home" in a Responsible Fashion

Phase One: Orientation

For the next week or so, do "Coming Home" within 45 minutes of waking up. Do this before you check for messages or contact any friends.

Brave Empath, this will help you to establish a sense of self that does not depend on your relationships with other people.

Take your time with the technique, allowing 90 seconds or more for each level. Be sure to write down your experiences.

After you come out of technique, read those notes. Then praise yourself for your courage as a skilled empath. Exploring your inner experience is so important during this phase of this Program for Empath Empowerment.

After completing "Coming Home" for that day, go forth and enjoy interacting with others. In the back of your mind, remember, it is safe to be yourself. You are allowed to have your own thoughts, feelings, physical sensations, etc. Basically, everything you used to do as an unskilled empath... you can do now... except for Split-Split-Second and Prolonged Empath Merges.

Phase Two: Familiarity with Yourself Grows

Over the next few weeks, or months, continue to do "Coming Home" every single day, preferably soon after waking up. It's helpful to get that going each day before you start talking to others.

This routine will help you grow more accustomed to being yourself, feeling comfortable that way. No extra pushiness or self-conscious attitude will be required. Automatically your sense of self will grow stronger.

In Phase 2, doing "Coming Home," you can shorten the amount of time you spend exploring most levels of self. With one important exception, it will be fine to spend just 30 seconds at each level: Social, Physical, Mental, Emotional, Spiritual.

That exception? Handle the timing a bit differently if you find one or more levels of self where you feel uncomfortable or go blank. Spend extra time there. Linger for a full 90 seconds or more.

As always, while doing "Coming Home," simply experience that level as you naturally do in the here-and-now. Don't try to pretty up your experiences or otherwise change a thing. Gently pay attention, then write something down. What about a level of self that you don't happen to enjoy right now? Scribble-write some words, as usual, e.g., "Grrrrrr, this stinks."

In general, when making your scribble notes during technique, let them be as honest as ever. Whatever you happen to notice, it is what it is. After ending the technique, read your latest notes in that spirit of interested self-acceptance.

During the rest of your waking hours, outside of technique, integration of your personality will continue rapidly.

Phase Three: Your Exploration Turns Downright Enjoyable

Brave Empath, your next phase in using the technique is based on experience: This new phase will begin when, for several day in a row, you have enjoyed every level of yourself while doing "Coming Home." Every single level.

Then you can cut the time for each level of "Coming Home" down to five seconds.

After you come out of technique, go about your day, more integrated than ever.

What's new at Phase 3, besides the shorter time spent at each level? You might start to add a few minutes of journaling to your daily routine. Quick little notes. They don't need to be fancy.

Do that journaling before you go to sleep every night. Summarize positive little discoveries about your human life that you made today, things accomplished in objective reality plus:

- How you reacted in a particular situation
- Things you did well
- Any new textures or qualities that were part of your personal experience that day

Brave Empath, you can expect to find that more and more about everyday reality fascinates you. Trust that this is healthy. Because, really, it is.

Non-empaths who have basic mental health have *always* been living this way.

Phase Four: Exploration Accelerates

Is that sense of yourself growing stronger? Then you can start decreasing the amount of time you spend at each level, day by day. Unless something happens on a particular occasion that is not enjoyable, in which case linger a while, exploring gently.

After some days, you might spend just a second or two at each level of self. And writing down scribble notes is no longer needed. Simply grab information as usual; put it in words as if you were writing things down. Noticing is enough now.

Consider this a graduation of sorts!

With your journaling at the end of the day, continue to write only positive things. That contrasts with thinking-type notes that you might make *during* the technique, which could be positive or icky or anything, really.

Both "Coming Home" and journaling in Phase 4 will help you to keep learning about yourself. Discover more every day about your quirky, individual sense of identity. Relish your varied experiences here at Earth School.

Phase Five: Graduate to Coming Home, Eyes Open

Brave Empath, advance to this phase of exploration only when you are feeling truly comfortable in your own skin.

By now you are used to waking up and noticing *yourself* first, not other people or ways to clean up your home or rushing to work. Yourself.

Not self-improvement or goals or religious obligations, either. You are yourself. Even if doing something related to self-improvement or goals or religious obligations, you are the doer. That's right, you don't disappear.

Overall, each new day here on earth is about you. Definitely allowed! Non-empaths have always lived that way. Now you can do that too.

Given this balanced way of life, it is appropriate for you to move to the Phase 5 Version of "Coming Home."

Early in your day, speak aloud the following sequence of sentences, substituting your name for "Henrietta" (unless you really are named Henrietta). Change some of the language if it makes you more comfortable. Because not everyone feels comfortable lavishing praise on yourself to such an extent, while some others of you empaths might wish to say something even more appreciative.

Love and gratitude for you, my human identity as Henrietta.

Love and gratitude for you, dear, precious body.

Love and gratitude for you, dear, precious mind.

Love and gratitude for you, dear, precious emotions.

Love and gratitude for you, dear, precious spirit.

I feel grateful that I am able to live this day as myself.

What else, Brave Empath? About that end-of-day journaling... continue it only if you find the practice enjoyable.

Phase Six: Over the Years, Deepen Your Experience

Whenever you like, repeat the previous five phases of exploration with "Coming Home." How often, exactly?

- Once a year might serve you. Or once every few years. Your choice.
- Sometimes you might go through rough patches on your journey through life. That could make it especially productive to repeat those five phases at a new level of personal growth.
- Or you might have a lovely spiritual awakening.
- Or you might even cross the threshold into Householder Enlightenment.

Brave Empath, feel free to restart the previous five phases for any reason. Or for no reason in particular.

Now you have the great combination, Brave Empath. Self-authority and skills, both. That's the ticket!

It is healthy to focus on yourself in this lifetime. You, a person who now happens to be a skilled empath.

CHAPTER 38

Ten Rules for a Skilled Empath

For your emerging comfort as an empath, a handful of rules can make a big difference. Of course, these are not coping tips nor are they a substitute for all that has gone before in this Program for Empath Empowerment.

Each of the following rules makes sense only if you have already gone through our previous chapters. Brave Empath, this has helped you to develop finesse at positioning your consciousness appropriately.

Empath skills are mostly about how you use your amazing gift of spiritual awareness.

Based on that, it is appropriate to explore some simple rules to make your life better. I know you can read them with an apprecia-tion of the consciousness factor.

Every born empath can live as a skilled empath if you will only follow these simple rules.

Skilled Empath's Rule One Do the "Coming Home" Technique Early Each Day

Each day at Earth School provides a new beginning. You can start fresh, doing what you wish, helping and learning, becoming what you want to be. Set the tone appropriately by doing "Coming Home" within 45 minutes of waking up.

Automatically this will turn your empath gifts OFF, positioning consciousness appropriately for all that follows in this new day.

Even that Phase 5 "Eyes-Open" quickie will suffice, once your skill has developed enough for this phase to be appropriate.

Skilled Empath's Rule Two. Use "Empath's First Aid" Appropriately

Enjoy the comfort this little technique can bring you. Just use it sparingly, and not as a substitute for the preventative help of "Coming Home."

"Empath's First Aid" will keep your energy field clear. It can also get you accustomed to feeling like yourself.

When is it a good time to use this technique? Out of nowhere, you notice a change in how it feels being you. And that change does not seem warranted by what has happened to you in objective reality. For example, no piano just fell from a window, missing you by inches. More likely examples follow:

- After hanging out with your friend Carlos, you literally feel a pain in the neck.
- While in a business meeting, you find it hard to know what you think. Other people's ideas and opinions seem overwhelming.
- Talking on the phone with your mother, you feel depressed. Before that conversation you felt just fine. And nothing your mother said was particularly depressing.
- At the gym, you start feeling as though your body is fat and blobby. (Regardless of the actual size and muscle tone of your physical body, which has not changed a great deal since you first entered the gym.)
- One look at your neighbor Zeke and you feel like a victim, not your usual way of living or feeling. Not at all.

Changes like these can definitely result from Split-Split-Second Empath Merges. But don't stop to analyze. Soon as you can find a private moment, do the "Empath's First Aid." If you feel better, you needed it. If nothing changes, you haven't sacrificed much time, have you? Consider those minutes an investment in your personal development.

You'll note however, Brave Empath, I have also recommended that you use Empath's First Aid sparingly. See our next rule to understand this more thoroughly.

Skilled Empath's Rule Three
Engage in Life, Not Incessant Self-Improvement

This Program for Empath Empowerment has given you many powerful techniques to turn your empath gifts OFF naturally, also ways to banish Imported STUFF. Use these appropriately. Don't make them your life. Let your life be about your life.

In particular, do not overuse "Empath's First Aid." Once or twice a day is fine. More than that and you may be compensating for patterns of STUFF that have nothing to do with Skilled Empath Merge.

For example, what if you feel depressed many times in a day? Maybe something happening now in your life triggers that reaction. Appropriately. Because a problem in objective reality warrants concern. Every negative feeling you have is not necessarily inappropriate.

The Serenity Prayer might apply to your situation: Change the things you can. Accept the rest. Develop skill at telling them apart, "the wisdom to know the difference."

Maybe one special person in your life is going through a patch of terrible difficulties. If that depresses you, it doesn't necessarily mean you are doing loads of unskilled empath merges. Life at Earth School is challenging. Do your reasonable best to be a good friend. Grieve privately when you must.

Maybe nothing is going wrong with your near ones and dear ones, and life externally seems to be fine. Despite that, you still might go through strong, negative feelings. Well, don't just keep doing "Empath's First Aid" all day long. And don't overuse other healing techniques either, like E.F.T. tapping sessions 20 times a day.

Instead, it might not hurt to get a medical checkup. Or sometimes a psychotherapist would be your best bet. Alternatively you might find a professional at mind-body-spirit healing whom you trust. Imported STUFF is not the only kind of energetic problem that could be limiting your life.

Skilled Empath's Rule Four
Refuse to Do Boredom

Brave Empath, having less Imported STUFF makes it all the easier to vanquish boredom. You possess unique ways to accomplish, to learn, to serve others. An amazing life awaits.

One common cause of boredom is not using your self-authority. Do things your way. Now! (Just remember to get skills for your chosen activities that require skill, not confusing self-authority with owning skills.)

Sorting out the difference between self-authority and skills will be all the easier for you now, given the clarity that results automatically from Empath Empowerment.

An extra resource for living large and lively rather than bored and brooding? Enjoy having your own natural, brilliant, amazing consciousness. Throughout your long history as a soul, you may have had some pretty fabulous incarnations. But never have you been given another incarnation exactly like this one. Nor will that identical chance ever come again. In that sense, the popular saying is true. "You" only live once. Celebrate YOLO.

One technique you have learned is especially helpful as a boredom buster. When you feel sooooo boooooooooooored and inwardly fidgety, do the "I Like" technique. Then find something else to do in objective reality.

"An idle mind is the Devil's workshop." So goes a pretty useful saying, even if (like me) you don't believe in a devil. There has to be more to life than sitting around, by yourself or with others, waiting until you get the munchies.

Skilled Empath's Rule Five
Avoid Recreational Chemicals

Another advantage of playing "I Like"? You can substitute that for mucking up your aura with big frozen blocks of STUFF, the inevitable result of taking recreational drugs like marijuana.

Sure, STUFF incurred from cannabis can always, always, always be healed. Still, life flows far better without recreational drugs messing up your consciousness and aura. Based on my work helping clients, here's my advice. What can you do in a social situation with a choice between alcohol and pot, when you feel like you'll burst if you don't get high one way or another?

Choose the booze.

Even a revolting episode of throw-up drinking, complete with horrible hangover the next day... has far less auric impact long-term compared to weed. Even a little fun with a reefer will put high-intensity frozen blocks into your energy field.

Granted, current social pressure (and sometimes even sanctimony) around smoking grass is so thick, it's almost enough to set off a smoke detector.

Mind-altering chemicals put STUFF into an aura in a way that alcohol doesn't. Sure, drinking kills brain cells; I don't particularly recommend it. Just saying, alcohol sure is preferable to the more subtle long-term effects on consciousness from psychoactive toys.

Incidentally, enjoying a glass of wine with your dinner will not counteract your authentic sense of identity, so important for continued growth as a skilled empath.

Skilled Empath's Rule Six
Take a Vigorous Interest in Your Human Life

Actively pursue relationships and hobbies, Brave Empath. Move forward in your work life, making it great. Automatically you will spend less time thinking about other people and what's wrong with them, replaying past conversations and dwelling on emotional pain.

Skilled Empath's Rule Seven
Reach out Daily

When possible, choose to visit people in objective reality. Real-life visits will enrich your consciousness and build social skills.

Texting, tweeting, and social networking cannot compare. Aura reading research clearly demonstrates that people evolve faster by being present with others in energetic real time, whether in the room, by phone, or webcam.

By contrast, electronic interaction done at random intervals? This directs consciousness in shallow ways.

Admittedly, shallow experiences can supply a different kind of fun. At least these electronic conversation are still done in objective reality, through voice or keyboarding or other ways of interacting electronically.

Can you appreciate how different all that is from wishing, hoping, thinking, praying, fantasizing, or other endless journeys into subjective life?

Skilled Empath's Rule Eight
Whenever You Have a Choice, Live in the Present

However you enjoy connecting to people, Brave Empath, choose to do it with your conscious mind rather than old habits of slip-sliding into unskilled empath merge.

It's perfectly normal to get lost in thought, occasionally. Eventually, though, you have a moment of choice.

Huh? You realize that you were just having an away moment. What to do then? Reinsert yourself into objective reality.

- Say something.
- Do something.
- Move your body.
- Use one or more of your senses.

Anything will do, so long as you engage with objective reality. Automatically your consciousness will shift, positioned in a way that is the opposite of drip-drip-drip. That consciousness of yours will be living in the present.

Skilled Empath's Rule Nine
Downplay Seeking Grand Purpose. Just for Now.

We empaths tend to be such idealists. We can long for something bigger than life's trivial little activities. Unfortunately, this can make us susceptible to joining cults, taking drugs, and other dangerous ways to jazz up humdrum human reality.

A related vulnerability is disregarding your life due to a valiant search for some grand purpose.

Brave Empath, have you been tormenting yourself unintentionally, seeking a grander, mystical purpose? Consider this. Creating demand for "Find your purpose" happens to be a very big business. Follow the money. Then you'll appreciate how easy it is for unscrupulous people to capitalize on the very human search to find meaning in life.

Truth is, most adults never find a flashy grand purpose. Because there may not be one.

Evolving at Earth School, finding human satisfactions, fulfilling ideals the best you can, and being of service to others — for most of us, that's It. Purpose enough. A pretty sacred purpose, actually.

Your life can also gain meaning by how you use your free will. Use it to set goals, choose interests, make new friends, evaluate the friendships you have now. Doing all this is hard work, but there's no substitute if you really want to grow spiritually.

Finding a fancier special purpose will not let you off the hook. Nor will it keep life on earth from being frustrating, confusing; sometimes downright ugly, sometimes beautiful.

Here is one way to grow super-fast as an empath. For your first year as a skilled empath — maybe starting right now — stop seeking your purpose. Just live.

You can still find plenty to keep you interested. More than if you have constantly been struggling to find some greater, higher, fancier, larger-than-life, official purpose.

Your newfound identity as a more skilled empath? This will be strengthened by saying and doing things, grand purpose or not. Be willing to live that human life and see where it gets you.

Skilled Empath's Rule Ten
Enjoy Your Life

It really is the only one you've got. (For this incarnation, at least.)

Paying attention to your life as though it mattered? This can get easier when taking one day at a time.

Brave Empath, you can expect interest in your human life to grow. Now you are free to explore it as a skilled empath. In recognition, I'm going to start calling you something new, EVOLVING EMPATH. (Short for "Rapidly Evolving Empath.")

You are growing so quickly now, moving forward more beautifully than ever along your path of personal development.

CHAPTER 39

Gifts Owned, Embraced, Managed, SKILLED!

Evolving Empath, you have so much to celebrate. Not only has this Program for Empath Empowerment done just what you were promised. In the process, you discovered a great deal about yourself. Just as extraordinary, you will continue to learn more every day about life outside your own skin and aura, objective reality.

When it comes to dealing with that objective reality...

Unskilled empaths are less effective than non-empaths. But skilled empaths are more effective than non-empaths.

Why would that be? Consider what has been happening with you.

Techniques You Can Use for the Rest of Your Life

You've got skills now, not just talent. This Program for Empath Empowerment has taught you:

1. How to use Vibe-Raising Breaths in everyday life. The technique called "Introduction to Vibe-Raising Breaths" can release some of the Imported STUFF in your aura that has resulted from unskilled empath merge. (Just be sure to include this powerful technique sparingly. Don't sprinkle it throughout your day. Let your life continue to be about your human life.)

2. The use of "Grounding Breaths" can help position your consciousness more appropriately in everyday life.
3. Installing "An Automatic Subconscious Alert" has begun to break the pattern of Prolonged Unskilled Empath Merge.
4. Teaming up with the Divine at will is so useful for techniques that involve consciousness (such as when you do "Get Big").
5. The "Empath's First Aid" technique, also to be used sparingly, provides instant help for Imported STUFF from unskilled empath merges.
6. "Coming Home" prevents the old drip-drip-drip.
7. Conscious ownership of your gifts helps you to respect yourself.
8. Embracing your magnificent sensitivity, you can rightly feel proud of being a Highly, Highly Sensitive Person, an empath.
9. Intellectually you can now clearly distinguish skill versus self-authority, honoring the latter while you develop the former, and using both resources to strengthen your sense of self.

Evolving Empath, congratulations on completing Step TWO of this Program for Empath Empowerment.

Actively Engage an Empath's Greatest Resource

Evolving Empath, what is that superb resource you have learned to engage? Your consciousness. You have begun using an effortless awareness of your own awareness. You have begun to purposely position awareness through conscious choice.

Not doing this often. Just doing it occasionally. And, at those times, doing it marvelously well.

Every one of the techniques you have learned works because of your magnificent consciousness, an empath's greatest resource.

Consciousness is abstract yet indispensable. Many of us living now, after The Shift that occurred in December 2012, are noticing energy more than ever. Humanity has moved into The Age of Energy — which brings us more interactions with astral-level energy than ever before in recorded history. By definition, astral (or psychic-level) experience is flashier than human anything.

By contrast, how about everyday, human frequencies? It takes a certain kind of humility to explore them. Yet living here at Earth School, your main job is being human.

Not only do you have the special assignment of being an empath. You are *human* while developing those empath skills.

Looking back at this Program for Empath Empowerment, you have learned how to use consciousness to help explore your humanity. Only the appropriate positioning of consciousness will turn empath gifts OFF: Positioning your consciousness at *human* frequencies.

Exploring flashy astral experiences or Divine-level sacred experiences? You have found an alternative. Explore human experiences first. Yours, not experiences belonging to random other people.

Spending time on non-human vibrational frequencies could be compared to eating chocolates. Fine for a treat, as part of a balanced diet. No substitute for a body's required nutrients.

Your sense of identity can grow strong only when you are willing to pay attention to human frequencies, to notice objective reality and solve problems through speech and action.

So why is it that skilled empaths are more effective than non-empaths, while unskilled empaths struggle through life with less effectiveness than the non-empaths?

Three reasons, seems to me.

#1. With Skills, You Prevent Imported STUFF

This is the first major way you have started to become more effective through this Program for Empath Empowerment.

All that Imported STUFF was subconscious, of course. Consciously you may not have noticed a big difference, having a new kind of energetic freedom from astral debris. Subconsciously, this change amounts to a very big deal. You have lessened the random STUFF entering your auric field multiple times each day.

Split-Split-Second Empath Merges weren't obvious to your conscious mind any more than the Imported STUFF that was deposited. Even Prolonged Unskilled Empath Merges weren't announced to your conscious awareness, as if trumpeted by a uniformed officer playing "Reveille."

Probably you didn't notice that drip-drip-drip entering your energy field, nor did you track all the accumulation, and its impact on daily life. Not consciously, anyway.

But now you can consciously appreciate the significance. What does it mean for everyday life, having less Imported STUFF?

- You become more effective at work.
- You can explore hobbies with more gusto.
- You are free to engage in social relationships with a stronger sense of identity.

Over time, all this growth will continue in cumulative fashion.

#2. Your Skills Help Other People Respect You More

It's ironic, I know. Evolving Empath, you could even call it sad. Doing all those unskilled empath merges, you used to help other people. Temporarily, it's true. And with icky consequences for your own aura. Still, you *were* helping people as a clueless kind of volunteer.

So it could be considered both sad and ironic that, previously, this caused problems for you. Clearly visible to everyone you have known, at a subconscious level, uh-oh! Imported STUFF was clinging to your aura like dirt on a car's windshield.

Junked up with this subconscious kind of debris, you couldn't see others so clearly. Nor could they see the real you.

Having less STUFF is helping you to become more attractive subconsciously. Others will respond to you better automatically. Better auric modeling!

Just think about your relationships lately. Hasn't there been an upgrade? Non-empaths, in particular, will respect you more.

To them, you probably used to seem a bit spaced-out. While now you seem to walk with your feet on the ground. Or call it "Driving through life with a way-cleaner windshield."

#3. With Skills, You Can Solve Problems Better

Evolving Empath, of course, you have always done your best to solve problems. But consider what I have learned from facilitating thousands of sessions with clients who are empaths.

Unskilled empaths try to solve problems with awareness.
Non-empaths use speech and action.
And so do skilled empaths.

For example, say that Frederick is your close friend. While you're talking on the phone one time, he seems preoccupied, distant.

As an unskilled empath, most likely you would have done a sequence of unskilled empath merges. Trying to figure out what was bothering him, all that flying in spirit might have informed you in a vague, subconscious way. Throughout the conversation, you would have kept at it, doing a kind of multi-tasking rather than normal conversation.

Now, being a skilled empath, you will not choose this way of solving problems. You're more likely to just ask the guy, "Hey, Frederick, you seem a little preoccupied. Is there anything bothering you?"

You know, talking. Asking questions. Dealing with what the other person says in reply.

Mind reading? Needing to check out other people subconsciously? This is not how human life is designed to work best.

Which is why problem solving, for humans, becomes far more effective when you play by the rules. Skilled empaths are more effective at life than unskilled empaths. Our extreme sensitivity helps us when we stay right on the surface of life.

We really can be more effective than non-empaths. And that's not even counting what happens after learning techniques for Skilled Empath Merge. Hint: High-quality inside information, safely and appropriately made your own.

More About Adding Skilled Empath Merge

Evolving Empath, wait as long as you like before doing Step THREE of this Program for Empath Empowerment.

The Master Empath, the sequel to this book, will coach you. Why choose to be coached? After all, that Step THREE is totally optional. You have done the far more essential Steps ONE and TWO in this Program for Empath Empowerment.

Only aren't you a bit curious about what empath gifts are for? Why did you incarnate with this kind of lifelong talent?

Empath talent doesn't help a person to solve human problems, particularly. It's no substitute for normal human communication or taking appropriate action. However, that hardly makes empath talent useless.

Skilled Empath Merge is a form of deeper perception. Actually, it is the ultimate form of deeper perception.

Don't you continue to be curious about what makes other people tick? I have a hunch you are curious in that way, more curious than most — even though now you're much better adjusted to being human.

Still, that old drip-drip-drip in our analogy came from an extra faucet. Extra goodies!

Since birth you have had an amazing talent for reading people deep down. Well, what's with that?

When your first priority is — rightly — to be healthy and happy, how can you satisfy that lifelong curiosity to learn more about other people?

A Brief Survey of Deeper Perception

Let's survey different ways to read people deeper. Which of them have you explored so far?

1. Shallow perception

It's only reasonable to begin our survey at the opposite of deeper perception. Which would be paying attention to objective reality

Pretty darned important! Pretty informative, too!

What does a friend like Frederick really do? Maybe he delivers what he promises. Maybe not. Maybe he treats you with respect. Maybe you used to be far too busy to notice.

Shallow perception can be tremendously useful. It is available to every normal human adult with average intelligence. Don't turn up your nose at it, Evolving Empath.

Could be that, now that you are a skilled empath, you will appreciate shallow perception more than ever. Without the distraction of unskilled empath merges, human speech and action become far more interesting and informative.

2. Theories about what makes people tick

Belief systems galore can help you to deconstruct reality, torque it, analyze it, shred it, play with the surface of life to your heart's content.

Whether you compare baseball statistics or analyze human motivation, theories about life are available to non-empaths as well as to you. Techniques abound, based on theories about the surface level of reality: Techniques to win friends and manipulate people, ways to gain success and prosperity.

Your belief system about what makes people tick may change over time, of course. I mean no disrespect to beliefs by pointing out the obvious: Theories allow shallow perception to be treated in an elegant manner. Shallow perception it remains, however, being based on what people say and do in objective reality. Evolving Empath, you can outgrow mere theories.

3. Expression reading

Once you open the door to reading expression and body language, it's hard to ever go back.

Right there, near the surface of life, those funny faces that people make actually *mean* something. Nonverbal communication indicates something deeper than the surface level of reality, and that can be quite a thrill to discover.

Maybe you still remember when you first learned to read body language. What a huge thrill that tends to be for an empath!

For non-empaths, expression reading may be plenty deep enough, even seeming almost too far-fetched and impractical. By contrast, all Highly Sensitive Persons tend to love this kind of exploration. We're naturals at it.

As for a Highly, Highly Sensitive Person like you — sure you're great at reading expression. But, honestly, does it satisfy you? You have so much talent for going still deeper.

4. Face reading for character

A deeper way to read people is physiognomy. For at least 5,000 years, professional face readers have interpreted physical data like ear angles and cheek proportions.

If you think that face reading means reading expression... some delightful surprises await. Face reading for character is entirely different. It is a much deeper form of perception than expression reading. This study may reward you with greater success at work, improved personal relationships, and more.

As with all the types of deeper perception that will be summarized in the rest of this chapter, it is important to know that gaining skill matters, and so does the system for teaching those dedicated skills. I have trademarked one system in this field, Face Reading Secrets®. The purpose is to gain detailed and practical information about character. In the background, the system is designed to boost the face reader's self-esteem and also open up greater compassion.

Other face reading systems aim differently, such as fortunetelling or diagnosing health problems or typing people.

Ever notice how many types of automobile exist in the world? By comparison, the field of physiognomy includes way more variety. Each school of face reading produces consequences for the knower, so use your discernment before committing to any particular system.

For empaths, physiognomy can be an excellent form of deeper perception. The resulting insights will be very human. As a side effect, noticing physical face data can prevent unskilled empath merge. You will stay right on the surface of that face, while checking out nostril shapes and lower eyelid curve.

5. Energy reading

Living now, in this Age of Energy, it is easier than ever to notice... energies. Highly Sensitive Persons (empaths particularly) have always had some awareness of energy, but now all humans are starting to notice it more.

Reading energy can include vibing out people, getting a gut feeling or intuitive hit, seeking inner guidance, seeing colors or lights around people, or simply knowing about somebody in a somewhat deeper way.

Does energy reading require doing empath merges, whether skilled or unskilled? Definitely not. READING ENERGIES simply means positioning consciousness toward the astral and subconscious frequencies built into life — especially effective when done as an intentional, attentional shift. And done with skill.

Since The Shift it has become easier for anyone to move awareness in this subtler direction. However, this is not necessarily done with skill. As you know, skills are learned. Skills do not spring up automatically due to self-authority, curiosity, or need.

So I recommend that you postpone energy reading until you have learned Skilled Empath Merge from *The Master Empath*. This part of the Program for Empath Empowerment offers you a more stable life than constantly alternating between the surface level of reality and various energies.

How refreshing! With your level of skill now, as an empath, noticing energies can become a conscious choice. Because all you need do is position awareness in the desired direction. Say that you are talking with a new colleague at work, Jeanette. What if you want to figure out whether you can trust her or not? You could:

1. Notice what she says and does. Surface-level human reality!
2. Monitor her expression while she talks to you, a skill set that comes naturally to human beings. Expression reading!

3. Quickly note an interesting facial characteristic. When experienced at physiognomy, you can rapidly interpret that face data. Not so experienced? Do your face reading in installments: Make a mental note of that one characteristic so you can look it up after returning home. Then re-engage in the conversation. (Maybe later you can find Jeanette's photo online and do a proper face reading along with your reference book, which could be even more useful.)
4. Check out Jeanette's vibes while you are talking. This would be energy reading or unskilled empath merge. Don't go there, Evolving Empath.

Why do I warn you to avoid random energy readings. Or even using a dedicated technique for Skilled Empath Merge, alternating with regular interactions? You would be dividing attention, multitasking with your consciousness.

To be sure, Jeanette will notice — subconsciously and maybe consciously, as well. This will not win you points with her. It is more likely to arouse suspicion.

Jeanette may not be an empath, but any person of average intelligence can feel when somebody else is doing something thing extra, rather than talking in a natural way.

Subconsciously, and maybe consciously, too, Jeanette will find "something about you" a little off-putting.

How can you bring yourself back to everyday ways of paying attention?

A simple shift of attention is all that's needed to avoid weakening yourself in the relationship. Tell yourself "Later." Then resume your normal conversation. Pay attention to that conversation — which just might, actually, teach you some interesting things about this person, Jeanette.

Fortunately, face reading and energy readings are not compulsions. They are skills.

As skills, they do not just happen to you. Evolving Empath, you choose whether or not to multi-task in these ways.

6. More sophisticated energy reading

After The Shift into this Age of Energy, everyone has become eligible to do some energy reading. How well you do it depends on whether or not you educate yourself about energy readings.

By way of analogy, everyone you know wears clothes in public, right? Outside of a nudist colony, anyway.

Some people wear whatever. Other folks pay a bit of attention to what they wear. Then there is Tim Gunn.

He's my favorite fashion expert. Okay, I skipped a category. Between paying a bit of attention to clothing, versus becoming a mega-fashionista like Tim Gunn, lies the relatively obtainable option of dressing well.

About energy reading, most folks are unsophisticated about what they're doing. I call this Stage One Energetic Literacy. With this kind of talent but lack of skill, the hunches are likely to be partly correct and partly incorrect.

Sorry. But it's true. Self-authority about reading energy does not automatically equate to skill.

Developing genuine skill is required to progress at energy reading.

1. One direction for study is psychic reading, which brings benefits like flashy perception and the support of mainstream New Age culture, which emphasizes The Romance of the Astral.
2. A different direction for study is Energetic Literacy, which I teach to empaths and non-empaths alike. In my experience, everyone who desires to learn these skills for aura reading can be successful.
3. Each system for learning to read energy has consequences. So use your consumer smarts before you commit to one type of study rather than another.

7. The ultimate form of deeper perception, Skilled Empath Merge

Only available to empaths like you, this is the very deepest perception for human beings. Even people who are spiritually Enlightened. (And yes, I have taught this skill to people in long-term, high states of consciousness.) Evolving Empath, your entire life, you have been capable of learning Skilled Empath Merge.

You have been hardwired with soul-level gifts. These special gifts, now owned, embraced, and managed... can be used along with additional skills to reveal so much about what it is like, being another person.

Steps ONE and TWO have been accomplished now. This Program for Empath Empowerment has taught you skills for being safe, living vigorously and effectively.

Step THREE will include other skills, especially a variety of techniques for Skilled Empath Merge. When you are ready for that, meet me at the sequel to this book, *The Master Empath.*

Celebrate What You Have Accomplished

At every level of perception, it shows. From the depths of your chakra databanks to the surface of your behavior, your degree of empath skills definitely shows.

The absence of Imported STUFF, the clarity as you talk and walk and engage in the surface of human life — yes, your skill level shows.

- For those with the discernment to notice consciously, your empath skills show.
- For every human being you meet, subconsciously your new skills show.

Most important, this achievement on your path of personal development shows clearly to God. And to you.

Congratulations on your persistence in learning. Among the millions of empaths in the world, you have proven yourself a leader.

In objective reality, enjoy using your greater effectiveness.

Subjectively, you are set for a sweet adventure as well. Every day can awaken a stronger sense of identity. Fulfilling human discoveries will illuminate your path of personal development.

Evolving Empath, you have learned to own, embrace, and manage your special gifts. Guess what? You really do know how to live as a skilled empath.

CHAPTER 40.

Ten Empaths, Empowered

To coach empaths is to encounter the most wonderful stories. Here is a small sampling from my clients all over the world. In their own words, these 10 empaths will share what stands out for them, having developed Empath Empowerment.

1. An Australian Acupuncturist's Awakening

In retrospect it seems like my life was shaped in so many ways by being born an empath. I think of one major aspect and think, "That's the main one." Then another aspect of equal significance pops up.

I had actually read a fair bit of Rose's work for empaths, knew about it for a while. For a long time I was on the fence about whether it applied to me.

What settled the issue was beginning my practice as an acupuncturist.

One problem for me was those unskilled empath merges that are regularly performed until we become skilled. For me, in addition, this was complicated by doing my diagnostic process, which required close focus on my patients. I was doing LOTS of unskilled merges on some very sick people.

My health deteriorated with frightening speed, since I began experiencing all my patient's various ailments as if they were my own. I found myself with an unexpected new smoking habit, to boot.

This forced me to think seriously about whether or not I was an empath. As it turned out, I have most of the empath gifts a person can have, and many of them are very strong. While I appreciate them now, these many and powerful talents constituted a serious vulnerability for a new healer.

One incident sticks in my mind as my first really clear recognition of what it meant for me, being an unskilled empath.

After doing the "Empath's First Aid" technique for the first time, I was reveling in what felt like my first experience of just being me. No-one else's weirdness rattling around inside. Just me. At this point, I knew how to divest myself of other people's STUFF, but I didn't yet know how to avoid taking it on in the first place.

I went to a pharmacy and overheard the end of a conversation. It sounded like the woman at the counter had been trying to convince the pharmacist to give her strong painkillers. Evidently she didn't have a prescription and the pharmacist, believing her to be an addict, refused.

This woman passed me on her way out. Immediately I had a clear experience of merging with her. I felt the shocking contrast between my previous sense of self versus the desperate emotions seething inside an addict who has just been refused a fix. The physically ill feelings of a body suffering from drug abuse. The spiritual twistedness that drug abuse creates.

This overwhelming experience nearly made me vomit.

Worse still was the realization that quickly followed. *I had been doing exactly this with everyone I had ever met, my whole life.*

What was the only difference this time? My sense of contrast.

Since then I have increased in skill as an empath. Gradually my health has begun to return. The number of patients I can treat in a week is increasing as well. My work is no longer destroying my health. And I can be in public without suffering other people's traumas.

— Adam McIntosh, Acupuncturist, Canberra, Australia

2. A High-Powered Business Coach Discovers Inner Silence

Getting skills as an empath has dramatically altered the texture and feel of my everyday life. Before I even knew what an empath was, I was taking in all of this noisy information from the people around me.

It was a little like having my car stereo on SEARCH and having it go from channel to channel, tuning in and then switching, whenever I was with other people. I learned to ignore it, but like ignoring the radio in a small car, it was not so comfortable.

I had this dawning awareness that everyone in the world was not experiencing what I was experiencing, and I was surprised. We tend to assume that our gifts are not that interesting because everyone must have them. That turned out to be not true at all.

I embarked on a search of the Internet, trying to find out what the heck was going on with me. I got a lot of quacks and some very bad advice, until I found Rose.

When I wrote her, to sign up for the Empath Empowerment Workshop, here is a little bit of what I said:

"I found and read your book, *Empowered by Empathy*, and the top of my head spun around and wobbled back on, slightly askew . . .

"When I read your book I realized that in everything I have done I have used Intellectual Empath Ability and Emotional Oneness to guide my work. I just did not call it that.

"I have also had some very ungrounded, scary experiences of going down the rabbit hole with other people's strong emotions that worked as a vortex into which I got sucked and had to fight my way out.

"And then last year I realized that I had to get a handle on my feelings, as they were too much what other people felt. I needed to learn to only feel my own feelings. That sounded impossible to me until I read your book."

When I went to that Empath Empowerment Workshop, I had one of the happiest moments of my life. I felt internal silence for the first time in my memory.

When Rose taught us to turn the unskilled empath merges OFF, and I did this as part of an extra-intense group experience, it was as though peace descended into me and I was so incredibly grateful and happy.

The other remarkable thing was it was easy. Once Rose explained the steps of the "Coming Home" technique and made it very simple, it was just easier not to do those unskilled empath merges. Easier, quieter, happier, and more satisfying.

Now, I can pay attention to my human everyday life. I am less clumsy, distracted, and less tired from trying to block out the noise all the time.

My friends and kids and husband notice that I am more present and happier, and they feel better about their relationships with me. Without my doing all those unskilled merges, they are able to tell me themselves all the things they want me to know. They can keep to themselves the things they don't. And they don't have the odd feeling that "Michelle knows everything and has invaded their space."

Having learned how to do Skilled Empath Merges, sometimes I will do them, with the very simple steps of a dedicated technique, and this has been beautiful and educational. I can do these empath merges on purpose, when I ask permission and it is serving me and the other person to do so, and I am in and out and then I am able to go back to human life with gratitude.

It has actually made my skill as an empath much stronger to have learned to turn OFF the unskilled merges and only do the skilled ones. So, if anyone is worried that to have the skill you must let it run away with you, it's patently not true. You actually get better and better as you use your empath gifts more and more consciously.

— Michelle Auerbach,
Communications Consultant and Executive Coach;
Boulder, Colorado

3. A Skilled Empath Relishes the Texture in Her Teeth

As an empath I have Physical Oneness, which is very strong. I also have Spiritual Oneness. Before developing skills, life's been full of anxiety except when I've minimized contact with people or lost myself in things like books, work, etc.

I bought Rose's book for empaths back in March, and yes, wow, I've really started to fall in love with myself and the world.

I will never again be able to say "I'm bOOOred." It seems impossible that I ever could have been bored.

I have surfaces to my skin and texture in my teeth, an amazingly available mind, ever-changing feelings and ideas, shoes that make interesting spaces around my feet, a much better idea of the things that entertain me, some divine friends, and even the beginnings of a handle on Relationships With Other People. (Big hurrah on that one!)

I've gone through the book three times now and it deepens every time. It's like having a fresh sharp shower in good common sense, and it's been the most accelerated process of personal transformation I've ever undergone. In February I felt fogged, dull and stuck. Now I feel like me again.

So all that's been fun and challenging and relaxing... but this weekend something really amazing happened. I spent the whole day just in my own skin. No effort required, I was just inside my own skin all day.

I didn't know it was possible to feel such peace. Everything inside and around me was smooth, calm, and peaceful. It wasn't empty; I was getting on with everything and having a normal day — but in this encasement of my own skin and this feeling of complete wonderful peace stretching out as far as I could sense. It was stunning.

Why settle for a thimble?

I remember that Rose wrote somewhere that if you're asking the Divine for water, you might as well ask for it ocean-sized, because too many people ask only for enough to fill a thimble. I had a Lottery approach to that one. I thought "Well, all right, I'll ask for the ocean — might as well." But my expectations were thimble-sized.

Imagine ordering the ocean from Amazon and expecting it to arrive in one of their brown cardboard packages. Well, that was me. And the delivery turned up, and I opened the front door and yes, there's the ocean, right on the doorstep.

One thing about the ocean — it's quite big, and impossible to mistake it for anything else.

I'm so excited because I know this will become normal. Because that was just me with my empath gifts turned off. Also I'm excited because from that place I can actually connect with other people — not as "an empath" but as me.

Rose told me once that for non-empaths that sense of peace is normal. What an incredible idea. To me it seems like the best present I ever got in my life!

If I can live like that as standard and travel by choice out into the "other" then, YES, being an empath could become fun rather than a burden. And I never thought I'd say that and mean it.

— Amanda Flood, Tai Chi Instructor; Cambridge, England

4. Not Fixing, Just Living Ridiculously Well Here in Norway

Getting empath skills changed my life from feeling like a leaf in the wind — where I kept being blown into an emotional gutter. Gradually I have become a man who knows who I am, what I want, and how I want it.

For years I used to live in fixing mode, waiting to figure life out before I could begin living it. In this fixing mode, I read a huge number of books, attended so many workshops, and learned so many different techniques.

When I met Rose, finally I found what I had been searching for. Empath skills taught me how to protect myself, and without first needing to solve all the big questions in life.

What else didn't I need to do any more? Push people away. Isolate myself. Or constantly feel the need to fix myself.

Turns out, I can protect myself without needing to manipulate anything, just by positioning my consciousness a little bit differently. How awesome is that? No need to figure out everything else about life, but just reposition my focus!

After learning that I was an empath — which came as a huge shock — pieces started to fall into place. I'll admit, at first I didn't believe in the idea of being an empath. Sometimes I have trouble believing it still, and I'm not even absolutely certain which empath gifts I have. But in desperation, I tried Rose's Empath Empowerment techniques. Despite not believing, my life gradually shifted. How could I not notice that?

I noticed. As the months go by, I feel more and more like I understand the meaning of "Coming Home."

What do I believe now, definitely? My relationships have improved. I can visit people without feeling the old kind of emotional "cramp," where I felt forced to turn away and protect myself.

Constant worrying and other problems that burdened me? They have been falling away, too. At times I feel so passionate and juicy about my life, it's ridiculous!

— Astrit Wold, Social Worker; Oslo, Norway

5. A Revelation Like No Other for a Teacher in Singapore

It was a revelation like no other: That I was an empath and had the habit of merging in consciousness with random people, lifting their STUFF and making it mine.

No wonder I had spent my life avoiding people, running quickly back to the sanctuary of home. And no wonder energy shields had limited impact for me.

Reading Rose's book, I slowly began to understand... and soon I caught myself in action. At a meeting, I was sitting completely still and fully focused on the speaker. My own existence was totally forgotten; only the speaker existed for me. Catching myself, I broke the focus and felt a sudden relief.

I feared that the real cause of this was my not having a strong sense of self, and that was why giving my full attention to others came naturally to me. But then how could I develop that strong sense of self, as someone doing all those unskilled empath merges?

Understanding more about Empath Empowerment now, I realize that my sense of self was basically fine all along. I just lacked skills for turning my empath gifts OFF. Besides, it didn't help my sense of self when I was taking on all the Imported STUFF.

No wonder I blamed myself, and also blamed other people for sapping my strength. For good reason, after being with those people for a while, all I wanted to do was to get away.

The reason wasn't really their being a problem. Similarly the reason for my feeling overwhelmed was not that something was wrong with me. Nothing was deficient in my sense of self. I just needed empath skills to support my true sense of identity.

Becoming skilled as an empath, there have been many benefits to my life. I take an interest in people now, initiate conversations, and am able to spend longer periods with friends without feeling spent.

Recently, after an outing with two friends, I was pleasantly surprised to find myself still full of life when I got home. The old me would have had to retire early for the night.

Now, when I do go to bed, I am able to fall into a deep and peaceful sleep the minute my head touches the pillow!

I work more efficiently too, and I don't do tedium.

What else do I notice? In general, there is far more clarity. This helps me to set personal goals. As a skilled empath, I have so much more awareness of my life — and how I can continue improving it.

— Jeya Devi, Primary School Teacher; Singapore

6. Other People's Problems? No Longer My Problem

As a skilled empath, what really sticks out for me is how differently I handle people now, especially those with big problems in their lives.

When I was an unskilled empath I had a colleague who was questioning whether or not she wanted a divorce. Back then, I went home from work in tears and prayed for God to help her. How great was the anguish I felt over *her* decision about divorce? Mine was nearly as strong as hers.

And mind, I had never met her husband. Nor been married myself. And my parents aren't divorced, either.

What changed after I became a skilled empath? Here's one example. My music teacher told me that she was getting divorced. I made sympathetic noises and commiserated but did not have a conversation about it (although I could kind of see she was angling for one).

Six months later, we went out to a jazz show together. We laughed and joked about her ex-husband and my ex-boyfriend, because it seemed they had some similarities, actually. We had some deep conversation too, about revelations we'd had and our current views about romantic deal breakers.

What else is remarkable about this conversation? Despite the subject matter I didn't go home that night with any emotional pain. I felt happy that I had made a closer friend of her; I felt glad that we related to each other on the topic of breakups.

As for the original colleague, whom I cried my eyes out for? We haven't spoken in years.

More former problems, no longer my problem....

Another thing is poignant for me about when I was unskilled. Back then I very clearly made some people uncomfortable. On some level they surely knew that I was experiencing their mostly subconscious emotions and discomforts. This made our relationships stifling for them, even when I didn't say much.

For example, I used to be friendly with both the sister and the mother of an ex-boyfriend. They were very social and gregarious creatures who could charm anyone, and they were lovely.

However around me they struggled to maintain the facade of "Everything is fabulous, Darling." They resented me. Why? I was unable to pretend that I had no clue about their unhappiness (or latent alcoholism), finding myself completely unable to respond enthusiastically to statements they made that I felt to be untrue.

Another problem when I was unskilled? This one happened when others around me had a strong opinion and articulated it forcefully: I found it very hard to argue my case or present my own opinion.

When I was having this discussion through a medium such as emails, I would be fine. In person, though, I would be kind of stuck — seeing the argument from their point of view and knowing that I didn't agree with it, yet not able to put forward a coherent stream of my own thoughts.

In general, as an unskilled empath it was hard to be "myself" as I didn't really know who that was. I became so influenced by other people's dramas, with my ups and downs coming to match theirs. It wasn't until I became skilled as an empath that my sense of self became stable day after day, and I woke up in the same spirit, and the inner barometer of how my life was going became consistent.

Finally, before my becoming a skilled empath, it was also very easy to become codependent in relationships. I did have to break up with a woman who had become friends with me, back when I was unskilled.

Here's what happened. She didn't really take to my becoming skilled. When we were together she desperately tried to engineer our relationship back to how it used to be, which just made it wearying and tiring to be around her. Such a contrast to the rest of my life now, as a skilled empath!

She didn't understand why I no longer enjoyed (or vicariously experienced) all the drama she was having.

Before, because I was unskilled, I was constantly picking up random bits of her emotional pain. When experiencing my friend's situation from how she experienced it, I was responding and reacting from that position. Now though, I could relate to her without that. What did I find?

She was happy to just go in circles. Actually she had never listened to anything I suggested. I realized I wasn't enjoying the friendship and decided to walk away!

— Emily Turner, Psychology Student; London, England

7. Engineering My Life, Based on Having It Be MY Life

Empath skills have changed my life in many positive ways. But it was the concept of EMPATH, as used by Rose, which has been most important, allowing me to achieve a better sense of who I am.

It was a complete shock to me, learning that it was possible to have a direct experience of someone else, both consciously and subconsciously. Sure, I was aware of the word "Empath." But my understanding was limited. I thought I was just vicariously experiencing someone else's experiences.

Actually, at those times, I was also having those experiences subconsciously, too, in a direct and personal way (what Rose now calls "Prolonged Empath Merges"). Plus there were so many Split-Split-Second Unskilled Empath Merges. Between these two types of empath merge, I didn't notice how often I reacted to situations based on energies and emotions that weren't really my own.

With skills as an empath, my relationships are improving because I am now responding to social situations spontaneously as myself, not just reacting to the other person's energies. For example, the other day a colleague was telling me a story that was very emotional. I could feel the emotional charge, recognize it for what it was, and not claim ownership. I effectively said no inwardly and kept my empath gifts turned OFF.

The "Coming Home" technique has been especially helpful for me. I do it in the morning and it provides me with a baseline for how I feel throughout the day.

For me, Empath Empowerment is about developing a clearer understanding of who I am. It's about being the most important person in the room!

— Paul Romero, Electrical Engineer; Philadelphia, Pennsylvania

8. Where Did All Those Needy People Go?

Living as a skilled empath has become a way of life. Seldom do I consider the contrast with all those struggles that once were quite standard for me. It's not as though I congratulate myself, how amazing it is that now I routinely keep my empath gifts OFF.

Earlier this year I was reminded. I'd embarked on a project to de-clutter my home. This included going through a huge pile of old journals that I had kept for years.

When I picked up a journal from ten years back, oh, the angst! Pages and pages were filled with worries, my thoughts about other people.

Such mental turmoil I went through back then. How I interpreted all this worry was that I had to work hard to extricate myself from the claws of needy people.

Somehow I couldn't get away from them. It seemed that one needy person after another demanded attention.

Consequently I sought refuge journaling. On a regular basis I would spend hours retreating and regrouping, trying with pen and paper to figure out better ways to deal with one "terribly needy" person after another.

Only when reading this particular journal did I realize — with great joy — how far I'd come. Today I am not thrown off balance by other people's emotions, moods, and needs.

What made the difference? I'm convinced that the change has been mine, not anyone else's.

Perhaps they hadn't been so terribly needy after all... especially since I'm no longer falling into unskilled empath merge on a regular basis. Certainly I don't have to work hard at figuring out elegant ways to cope with other people's (alleged) incessant demands and insatiable needs.

All my empath skills have been acquired from Rose's book on Empath Empowerment. The skills required are subtle, even simple. While learning, I wasn't even sure that anything was really changing.

Reading that journal made me appreciate just how much more energy and focus are available to me — now that I can be myself more fully. No more inhabiting the needs of other people. Now I fill my own space.

— Rachel Murdoch, Teacher; London, England

9. Empath? So That's What It Is.

Growing up, I discovered I was sensitive. For a boy that was considered a bad thing — a weakness, not a strength. Avoidance was the most effective strategy I found, although that was hardly a good life skill. Later I was startled to read, in one of Rose's books, how empaths often learn to be invisible. That was the story of my youth!

However, until I went to a conference in my 50's, I was oblivious to being an empath. In one session, they had us do an empath quiz. I was surprised to get a high score. But when I read the speaker's material later, she only covered a couple of empath gifts and I couldn't relate to them. So I had some information but nothing I could work with. I certainly didn't gain any skills or insight.

Skip forward some years and I ran into Rose Rosetree's work. Her Book One in the Empath Empowerment Series brought me a series of personal revelations. I discovered that I have multiple empath gifts, and that some of them were on all the time.

Once I became more conscious of my empath gifts, I was taken aback to discover I was constantly "reading" others. Previously I had no idea I was doing this. I also had no idea how to dial it down, let alone OFF. OFF was completely unfamiliar. In experience, I had no reference point for it.

Ironically, all this "reading" was largely subconscious, so it was not adding anything to my interpersonal skills. Since childhood, I subconsciously had my antenna up all the time, checking if others were OK or safe.

In retrospect I appreciate this didn't help anyone. Especially when I was concurrently trying to be invisible! Mostly the effect was stressing me out, as I soaked up anxiety and other energies of people around me.

While not recognizing I was doing this, I was very aware of some of the effects; things I largely attributed to personal deficiencies. Like how I adapted to work environments and became a different person on the job. Then how I struggled to not carry that home with me. I also see now how this affected many of my life choices.

Once I learned about the importance of empath skills, I was rather astonished that I had understood so little about my gifts. But thinking back on it, I recognize why.

I was born with those empath gifts and lived with them all along. Not having grown into those talents, I felt no shift that would have allowed me to recognize them. Life as an empath was just part of how I experienced my world from day one. Now I'm shifting from random reader to skilled empath, thanks to Rose. What a relief!

— David Buckland, IT Consultant; Vancouver, Canada

10. The Problem Was Never My Boundaries. It Was Talent

For most of my life... therapists, teachers, friends, so-called friends, tarot readers, psychics... kept telling me that I did not have good boundaries.

They all suggested things I could do to have better boundaries... so that I would not be adversely affected by other people, certain kinds of plants, grocery stores, airplane rides.

The list was extensive... parties, motel rooms, books, etc.

I spent thousands of dollars on spiritual candles, salt and soda baths, crystals, smudging practices.

I imagined all kinds of bubbles around me.

I used aromatherapy.

Oh, the list is endless.

Bottom line? Until I learned to be a skilled empath, my life consisted of mostly trying to stay away from people and things.

Rose's system of Empath Empowerment® has allowed me to have a more relaxed and comfortable life. And compared to all the other complex gyrations I went through in order to feel safe in the world? This is simple, straightforward, and permanent.

I now use my empath abilities to help others. Now I see being an empath as the gift it really is… instead of the curse that I used to think it was.

— Linda Stone, Rosetree Energy Spirituality Practitioner; Carlsbad, New Mexico

Acknowledgments

Enthusiasm from my students motivated me to write the first book for empaths *Empowered by Empathy*. Even more enthusiasm led to this series of Empath Empowerment® books.

The pattern is simple: Students keep teaching this teacher.

As a teacher of personal development since 1970, I get it by now. The more I teach, the more I learn. Every success at helping readers furthers my resolve to help whenever and however I can, while maintaining integrity.

By now I'm convinced that, more than anything else I have been given to teach, empath skills help people to live with a deeper spiritual awareness. I have been amazed and humbled at how well my students have done.

After one workshop, it took a week for me to recover from just how well they did. Since the techniques had been a real stretch for me to develop, I expected my students would struggle at least a little. As if! The learning came easily to them, a far cry from my earnest efforts to teach them.

It's as though I had been a mother bird pushing little ones out of the nest, anxiously hoping my fledglings wouldn't have too much trouble working their wings. Instead they stretched and sailed so easily, exploring like the birds they were born to be. And as we all flew together, I heard them chirp to each other, "That nest was okay but, hey, didn't it seem a little confining?"

So, who taught this teacher, who sometimes struggles and other times feels like a proud nest emptier?

Let's start with my husband, Mitch Weber. No other person has understood me so well, accepted me so thoroughly, supported me so generously. Any success I have as a teacher is really *our* success.

What else? The naming of deep experiences was required for me to bring forth this system. Until you dare to trust the outer reaches of your perception, naming cannot progress. So I honor Rev. AlixSandra Parness and the late Rev. Rich Bell, both of them instructors in Teaching of the Inner Christ (www.teachingoftheinnerchrist.com), for modeling spiritual trust. This led to my ability to name empath gifts, experiences, and techniques.

Around the same time that I studied with AlixSandra and Rich, in 1985, Susan Kingsley-Rowe facilitated my first past-life regression. I revisited being among the multitudes who heard The Sermon on the Mount. Or its equivalent... since the experience hardly came complete with a theater marquee.

The chiming presence of Jesus re-awoke in my consciousness. Under Susan's expert guidance, I remembered more about what I learned, privileged like so many of us back in the day, learning all we could from him.

Ever since, it has seemed to me that one of the ways Jesus used to help people was this: Connected to Spiritual Source, he would fly in spirit into the energies of those who asked for help. Joining fearlessly, joyously, fully, and fully supported. Empath merge of this kind was appropriate to the energies of that long-ago era, The Age of Faith.

A dozen years after exploring that past-life regression, I was inspired to write the first book for empaths. Many years after that was published, I listened again to the sound recording made by Susan Kingsley-Rowe.

Only then did I intellectually make the connection. Both empath gifts OFF and Skilled Empath Merge had been modelled for me way back then. With Susan's help, in depth hypnosis, I remembered how such a thing could be done.

My hunch is that this long-ago learning was carried forward into this lifetime, dormant until the memory was awakened. This inspiration is what made it possible for me to develop a variation on empath skills that would be suitable for our Age of Energy: How to safely live as an empath and, as appropriate, facilitate Skilled Empath Merge.

Other acknowledgements are due. So many teachers, healers, and students — definitely from this lifetime — have helped me to develop the system of Empath Empowerment. Indirectly, every one of you has helped to refine my empath talent. Even if space here does not permit my acknowledging all of you by name, my soul bears the imprint of every one of you. It is my privilege to carry your legacies forward.

One among you just has to be singled out, though. It's my most amazing college professor, at Brandeis University in the 1960's: Dr. Allen Grossman. This highly regarded poet used to tell us about a poet's job. And what was that job? To find the special excellence of a person or a place, then to express it with a true name.

Naming as a sacred process? Definitely possible.

The search for true names has taken me through poetry and religion, healing and metaphysics, relationship after relationship, and into finding language to coach empaths.

Acknowledging this long journey brings joy and plenty of other emotions as well. Back when I wrote *Empowered by Empathy*, I flashed on a bitter memory.

For 22 years after college I followed an Indian mystic, placing him on such a pedestal that I believed he was my only guide to Enlightenment. As a disciple, my life was devoted to teaching at his meditation centers. Studying directly with him for extended retreats, I would wait outside his door for hours on end, seeking in vain for a personal audience.

In all those years he granted me exactly one. Just one conversation. It lasted less than four minutes. At the end, I asked about prayer. "Please, teach me how to pray," I implored. My guru laughed long and hard. "Find it in a book" he said, turning away.

That memory burned for years because I heard contempt in his laughter. Hours of daily meditation, devoted service as a teacher, seven years of celibacy, work upon work and tears upon tears, despite all that — and in spite of all I had learned from my parents and teachers before him — would I always be such a fool that I didn't even know how to pray?

As I wrote my first book for empaths and sealed it with my thanks, I realized how my techniques to fly in spirit, through empath skills... how that could be considered a form of prayer. I heard my guru's laughter again. Only now I could hear the love in it. Could it be that he foresaw and, in a twinkling, fore-read *this book*?

Evolving Empath, I'm so glad I found it and you did, too.

— Rose Rosetree, Sterling, Virginia, May 2014

Share Your Experiences, Evolving Empaths

Easy to get and effortless — that's your new set of empath skills.

Do you know what can be hard to get? Book reviews.

Here is where you can help, Evolving Empath. Please write a review of this book, then share it at Amazon.com, barnesandnoble.com, goodreads.com, and any other book review websites you know. Even a couple of sentences can make such a difference for other empaths.

You'll also be giving back to this indie publisher, who strives to bring innovation to spiritual self-help... and do it with integrity.

What else? So many of you empaths have wonderful stories like those you've read here. They might be perfect for my future books or at the blog "Deeper Perception Made Practical."

I would love to read your tales of triumph. Send them to Rose Rosetree, 116 Hillsdale Drive, Sterling, VA 20164. Email to rose@rose-rosetree.com

It is so exciting. You are among the pioneering empaths in the world to develop these powerful skills. It has been such an honor to guide you through this Program for Empath Empowerment.

Evolving Empath, I wish you such happiness!

CPSIA information can be obtained
at www.ICGtesting.com
Printed in the USA
LVOW13s0350081017
551624LV00001B/9/P